Flutter for Mobile Apps Create Stunning Apps for Android and iOS

A Complete Guide to Building Cross-Platform Apps with Flutter

MIGUEL FARMER

RAFAEL SANDERS

All rights reserved

Table of Content

TABLE OF CONTENTS

INTRODUCTION

Unlocking the Power of Flutter for Mobile App Development

In the ever-evolving world of mobile app development, choosing the right framework is paramount to building successful, scalable, and high-performance apps. Over the past few years, **Flutter**, Google's open-source UI toolkit, has emerged as one of the most popular and powerful frameworks for building cross-platform mobile apps. With its ability to create beautiful, natively compiled applications for **iOS**, **Android**, **web**, **desktop**, and **embedded devices** from a single codebase, Flutter is revolutionizing how developers approach app development.

This book, *Flutter for Mobile Apps: Create Stunning Apps for Android and iOS - A Complete Guide to Building Cross-Platform Apps with Flutter*, is designed to equip you with the knowledge and skills needed to build high-quality mobile apps using Flutter. Whether you are a beginner just starting your Flutter journey or an experienced developer looking to deepen your expertise, this book covers everything you need to know about Flutter app development.

Why This Book?

As a mobile app developer, mastering Flutter will significantly streamline your development process. With **Flutter**, you can use one codebase to target multiple platforms, reducing development time, effort, and cost. In addition to the **core Flutter framework**, this book introduces you to best practices, state management techniques, and advanced topics like **networking**, **local storage**, **animations**, and **Firebase integration**. By the end of this book, you will be capable of developing sophisticated, polished mobile applications that provide a seamless user experience across platforms.

Flutter is widely recognized for its flexibility, performance, and ease of use. This book takes a comprehensive approach, walking you through the entire app development lifecycle, from setting up your development environment to deploying your app for the real world. The chapters are structured to guide you from basic concepts to more advanced techniques, ensuring that you build a solid foundation before tackling complex real-world scenarios.

What Will You Learn?

In this book, you'll explore the fundamental principles of Flutter development and take an in-depth look at how to:

- **Set up your development environment** for Flutter on **Windows**, **macOS**, and **Linux**.
- Learn **Dart**, the programming language used in Flutter, and understand how to write clean, efficient code.

- Master **Flutter widgets**, the building blocks of Flutter applications, and how to use them to create responsive, interactive UIs.
- Implement **state management solutions** such as **Provider**, **Riverpod**, and **Bloc** to manage app data effectively.
- Integrate **networking** functionality to communicate with APIs, fetch data, and display it in your app.
- Store data securely using **local storage** techniques like **SQLite** and **Flutter Secure Storage**.
- Create engaging **animations** to add life to your app and improve the user experience.
- Add advanced features like **push notifications**, **Firebase authentication**, and **cloud storage**.
- Build, test, and **deploy apps** for both **Android** and **iOS**, and even expand to **web** and **desktop** platforms.

Why Flutter?

Flutter's rise to prominence is no accident. Here are some key reasons why Flutter has become the framework of choice for many mobile developers:

- **Cross-Platform Development**: Flutter allows you to write a single codebase that runs on **iOS**, **Android**, **web**, **desktop**, and even **embedded devices**. This not only saves time but also ensures consistency across different platforms.

- **Beautiful UIs**: With its powerful set of built-in widgets, Flutter makes it easy to create visually stunning apps with smooth animations and custom designs that feel native.

- **Performance**: Flutter compiles to **native ARM code** and offers high performance compared to other cross-platform frameworks like React Native. This ensures your app performs as well as if it were developed natively.

- **Growing Ecosystem**: Flutter has an active community of developers and contributors, and its ecosystem of packages and plugins is rapidly growing, enabling you to integrate functionality like authentication, payments, and location services easily.

Flutter also stands out for its **hot reload** feature, allowing you to instantly see changes in your app without restarting the whole process, which accelerates the development cycle.

Who Should Read This Book?

This book is suitable for a wide range of readers:

- **Beginners**: If you're new to Flutter and mobile development, this book will introduce you to the core concepts and tools you need to start building apps from scratch. We explain every concept in simple, easy-to-understand terms, with plenty of examples and step-by-step instructions.

- **Intermediate Developers**: If you have some experience with Flutter but want to deepen your understanding and build more sophisticated apps, this book provides valuable insights into advanced topics such as state management, Firebase integration, and testing.
- **Experienced Developers**: For seasoned developers familiar with other frameworks, this book offers a detailed exploration of Flutter's features and best practices. It also highlights Flutter's performance advantages and teaches you how to leverage the full potential of the framework.

How This Book is Structured

The book is divided into **27 chapters**, each covering a specific aspect of Flutter development. You'll begin with an introduction to **Flutter** and **Dart**, followed by a detailed setup of your development environment. The chapters progress logically, with early sections focusing on Flutter's UI and basic widgets, and later sections diving into more advanced topics such as **state management**, **networking**, and **testing**. The final chapters provide you with real-world examples, including a complete **task manager app** and the process of **deploying** your Flutter app to the app stores.

Here's a quick overview of the chapters:

1. **Introduction to Flutter**: Learn what Flutter is and why it's a great choice for mobile app development.
2. **Setting Up Your Development Environment**: Get your development environment ready for Flutter and Dart.
3. **The Fundamentals of Dart**: Understand Dart, the programming language behind Flutter.
4. **Flutter Widgets – The Building Blocks**: Learn about Flutter's widget tree and the building blocks for creating UIs.
5. **Flutter UI Design – Building Beautiful Interfaces**: Design stunning UIs using Flutter's Material and Cupertino widgets.
6. **Navigating Between Screens**: Master navigation and routing in Flutter apps.
7. **Managing State in Flutter**: Learn about state management solutions like Provider, Riverpod, and Bloc.
8. **Networking and HTTP Requests**: Fetch data from APIs and manage network requests in your app.
9. **Local Storage and Databases**: Learn how to store data locally using SQLite and Flutter Secure Storage.
10. **Flutter Animations – Making Apps Come to Life**: Add beautiful animations to your app.
11. **Handling User Input – Forms and Validation**: Implement forms and validate user input.

12. **Managing App Life Cycle and Resources**: Understand app life cycle and resource management.

13. **Implementing Push Notifications**: Add push notifications to your app using Firebase Cloud Messaging.

14. **Integrating with Firebase – Firebase Essentials**: Use Firebase for authentication, real-time databases, and cloud storage.

15. **Building and Deploying Apps for Android and iOS**: Build and deploy your app to the app stores.

16. **Working with Geolocation and Maps**: Integrate location-based features with maps and geolocation services.

17. **Flutter for Web and Desktop**: Expand your app to web and desktop platforms.

18. **Testing in Flutter – Ensuring Quality**: Learn how to write unit tests, widget tests, and integration tests for your Flutter apps.

19. **Debugging and Performance Optimization**: Improve app performance and debug issues.

20. **Customizing Flutter Widgets and Themes**: Create custom widgets and themes to match your app's design.

21. **Accessibility in Flutter – Making Apps Inclusive**: Make your app accessible to all users, including those with disabilities.

22. **Advanced State Management – Provider, Riverpod, Bloc**: Deep dive into advanced state management techniques.

23. **Using Third-Party Packages and Plugins**: Integrate third-party plugins and packages into your app for added functionality.

24. **Security Best Practices in Flutter Apps**: Learn how to secure your app and protect sensitive user data.

25. **Internationalization and Localization**: Make your app available in multiple languages and regions.

26. **Real-World Case Study: Building a Full-Featured App**: Build a fully functional task manager app combining everything learned.

27. **Future of Flutter and the Mobile Development Landscape**: Understand the future of Flutter and how it's shaping the mobile development world.

Conclusion: Unlock Your Potential as a Flutter Developer

By the end of this book, you will have mastered the essentials of **Flutter development** and be equipped with the tools and knowledge to create beautiful, performant apps for iOS, Android, web, desktop, and beyond. Whether you're looking to build your first app or enhance your existing skills, this book will be your comprehensive guide to becoming a proficient and confident **Flutter developer**.

Let's dive in and start building the apps of the future with Flutter!

CHAPTER 1

INTRODUCTION TO FLUTTER

What is Flutter?

Flutter is an open-source framework developed by Google for building natively compiled applications for mobile, web, and desktop from a single codebase. It enables developers to create high-performance apps that look and feel native on both Android and iOS platforms. Flutter uses the Dart programming language, also developed by Google, and allows developers to build rich, interactive, and beautiful user interfaces (UIs) with minimal effort.

One of the key features of Flutter is its "hot reload" capability, which allows developers to see code changes in real-time without restarting the app. This feature speeds up development and debugging, making Flutter an attractive option for both new developers and experienced app creators.

Flutter provides a rich set of customizable widgets and tools to build visually appealing and smooth applications. By using Flutter, developers can create high-quality apps without sacrificing performance, which is a crucial factor when targeting mobile devices.

Why Choose Flutter for Mobile App Development?

1. **Cross-Platform Development**: Flutter allows you to write a single codebase for both Android and iOS applications. Unlike traditional development, where separate codebases are needed for each platform, Flutter eliminates the need for such duplication, saving time and effort.

2. **Faster Development**: Thanks to features like "hot reload," Flutter allows developers to see immediate changes without restarting the app. This dramatically reduces the time spent on testing and iteration, speeding up the development process.

3. **Native Performance**: Flutter apps are compiled directly to machine code, which means they offer the same level of performance as native apps built in Java or Swift. This is a significant advantage compared to other cross-platform frameworks that rely on intermediate code.

4. **Rich UI and Customization**: Flutter comes with a wide variety of pre-designed widgets that follow Material Design for Android and Cupertino for iOS. This enables developers to create highly interactive, visually appealing, and responsive UIs without writing excessive custom code.

5. **Growing Community and Ecosystem**: As an open-source framework, Flutter has seen significant adoption from the development community. With a growing set of

17

plugins, libraries, and tools, developers can easily add new features to their apps without reinventing the wheel.

6. **Cost-Effectiveness**: Since you can maintain one codebase for both Android and iOS, Flutter helps reduce development costs. This is especially beneficial for startups or small businesses that need to release their apps on multiple platforms quickly and affordably.

Flutter vs. Other Frameworks (React Native, Xamarin, etc.)

When considering Flutter, it's important to compare it with other popular mobile app development frameworks, such as **React Native** and **Xamarin**.

- **Flutter vs. React Native**:
  - **React Native** uses JavaScript and React to build mobile apps, and it relies on native components for rendering. While React Native allows for cross-platform development, its performance can sometimes fall short compared to Flutter, which compiles directly to native code. Additionally, React Native's UI components are often more reliant on native code, which can lead to platform-specific variations.
  - **Flutter**, on the other hand, uses its own rendering engine to create UIs, which ensures a consistent look and feel across platforms, with less reliance

18

on platform-specific components. It is also faster in terms of performance due to its native compilation.

- **Flutter vs. Xamarin**:
  - o **Xamarin** is another cross-platform framework that uses C# and .NET to build apps. While Xamarin also allows for code reuse across Android and iOS, it often requires more platform-specific code and does not provide as seamless an experience as Flutter. Xamarin also struggles with performance in certain scenarios due to the need for a Common Language Runtime (CLR).
  - o **Flutter**, however, uses Dart and avoids the need for a runtime, which leads to more efficient apps. Flutter's rich ecosystem of widgets, as well as its ability to maintain visual consistency across platforms, makes it an attractive alternative to Xamarin.

Overall, while React Native and Xamarin are both excellent choices for mobile app development, Flutter's unique approach to building UIs and its focus on performance give it a significant edge in many cases.

Overview of Flutter's Architecture

Flutter's architecture is centered around a **reactive framework** that uses a **widget-based UI**. Understanding Flutter's architecture will give you insights into how it handles rendering, events, and data flow.

Here are the core components of Flutter's architecture:

1. **Dart Virtual Machine (DVM)**:
   o Flutter is built on the Dart programming language. The Dart VM executes code in both the development environment (JIT, Just-in-Time) and production (AOT, Ahead-of-Time), which allows Flutter to perform efficiently during development and once deployed on a user's device.

2. **Flutter Engine**:
   o The Flutter engine is a low-level runtime that provides the necessary support for rendering, input events, and networking. The engine is responsible for Flutter's custom rendering system and includes libraries for rendering text, images, and animations.

3. **Framework**:
   o Flutter's framework consists of a wide range of pre-built **widgets** that developers can use to build

their app's UI. The framework handles much of the boilerplate code and allows developers to focus on app logic.

o   Flutter's widgets are layered in a hierarchy, with **stateless** and **stateful** widgets being the building blocks. The framework is designed to be flexible and easily customizable, ensuring that developers can create highly interactive and dynamic UIs.

4. **Widgets**:

o   Every part of a Flutter app, from the layout to the controls and even the text, is a widget. Widgets are the core element of Flutter's UI, and they are classified as **stateless** or **stateful** based on whether they maintain any mutable state.

5. **Rendering**:

o   Flutter uses its own rendering engine, which is built on **Skia**, a powerful graphics library used for 2D graphics rendering. This engine allows Flutter to draw UIs directly onto the screen, providing high-performance rendering even on complex UIs.

6. **Platform Channels**:

o   Flutter uses platform channels to communicate with native code, such as Java (for Android) and Swift (for iOS). This allows developers to access platform-specific features not directly available in Flutter's framework, making it possible to interact with APIs or hardware features like sensors and cameras.

How Flutter Works: Widgets and the Flutter Engine

At its core, Flutter is all about **widgets**. Everything in a Flutter app is a widget—whether it's a button, an image, or a padding layout. These widgets are organized into a **widget tree**, which is a hierarchical structure of widgets.

- **Stateless Widgets**: These are widgets that do not change over time. They are static and do not have any internal state that changes during the app's lifecycle. Examples include `Text`, `Icon`, and `RaisedButton`.
- **Stateful Widgets**: These widgets are dynamic and can change their appearance based on user interactions or data changes. For example, a button that changes color when clicked or a list that updates based on new data.

The **Flutter engine** is responsible for rendering these widgets to the screen. The engine uses a **frame rendering system** that redraws the screen frequently to ensure smooth animations and transitions. It also allows for high-performance rendering and complex animations that feel native to both iOS and Android.

Flutter's use of **hot reload** helps developers instantly see changes to the UI, which speeds up the development and iteration process.

22

This chapter sets the foundation for the rest of the book. It provides readers with a clear understanding of what Flutter is, why it's a great choice for mobile app development, and the key concepts that power Flutter's architecture and rendering system. The real-world comparisons with other frameworks will help readers make an informed decision when choosing a framework for their next project.

CHAPTER 2

SETTING UP YOUR DEVELOPMENT ENVIRONMENT

In this chapter, we will walk you through the steps of setting up your development environment to start building Flutter apps. Whether you're on Windows, macOS, or Linux, you will learn how to install Flutter, set up the necessary tools, and configure your first Flutter project.

Installing Flutter on Windows, macOS, and Linux

Before diving into building apps, you need to install Flutter and set up your environment. The process for installing Flutter is slightly different depending on your operating system, so let's cover each one in detail.

Installing Flutter on Windows:

1. **Download Flutter SDK:**
   - o Go to the official Flutter website: flutter.dev.
   - o Download the latest stable Flutter SDK for Windows.

24

- Extract the zip file to a location on your machine (e.g., `C:\flutter`).

2. **Update System Path:**

   - Open **Environment Variables** by searching for it in the Start Menu.

   - Under **System Variables**, find the `Path` variable and add the full path to the `flutter/bin` directory. For example, `C:\flutter\bin`.

3. **Install Git:**

   - Flutter uses Git to manage its code. If you don't have Git installed, download and install it from git-scm.com.

4. **Run Flutter Doctor:**

   - Open a terminal or command prompt and run:

   ```bash

   flutter doctor
   ```

   - This command checks your environment for any missing dependencies and shows you instructions on how to resolve them.

5. **Install Android Studio:**

   - Flutter requires Android Studio to build and run Android apps. Download and install Android Studio from the official site: developer.android.com/studio.

o   Once installed, open Android Studio and ensure the Android SDK and Android Virtual Device (AVD) are installed.

Installing Flutter on macOS:

1. **Download Flutter SDK:**

    o   Go to flutter.dev and download the latest stable release for macOS.

2. **Install Xcode:**

    o   Open the **App Store**, search for **Xcode**, and install it.

    o   Once installed, run the following command to ensure Xcode is correctly set up:

    bash

    ```
    sudo        xcode-select        --switch
    /Applications/Xcode.app/Contents/De
    veloper
    ```

3. **Install Homebrew (if not installed):**

    o   Homebrew is a package manager for macOS that helps in installing dependencies. To install it, run the following in your terminal:

    bash

```
/bin/bash    -c    "$(curl    -fsSL
https://raw.githubusercontent.com/H
omebrew/install/HEAD/install.sh)"
```

4. **Update System Path:**

   o Add Flutter to your PATH. Open a terminal and add the following to your .bash_profile or .zshrc (depending on the shell you use):

   ```
   bash
   ```

   ```
   export
   PATH="$PATH:`pwd`/flutter/bin"
   ```

   o Apply the changes:

   ```
   bash
   ```

   ```
   source ~/.zshrc
   ```

5. **Run Flutter Doctor:**

   o Open your terminal and run:

   ```
   bash
   ```

   ```
   flutter doctor
   ```

   o This will check for any missing dependencies or issues.

Installing Flutter on Linux:

1. **Download Flutter SDK:**

   o Visit flutter.dev and download the latest stable release for Linux.

2. **Install Dependencies:**

   o Use the following command to install dependencies needed to build Android apps:

   ```bash
   sudo apt-get install -y curl git unzip xz-utils zip
   ```

3. **Update System Path:**

   o Add Flutter to your PATH by adding the following line to your ~/.bashrc or ~/.zshrc:

   ```bash
   export PATH="$PATH:`pwd`/flutter/bin"
   ```

   o Apply the changes:

   ```bash
   source ~/.bashrc
   ```

4. **Run Flutter Doctor:**
   o Open a terminal and run:

   bash

   flutter doctor

   o This will ensure all necessary components are set up.

Installing Android Studio & Xcode

Flutter relies on Android Studio for Android development and Xcode for iOS development. Let's dive into installing these tools.

Installing Android Studio:

1. **Download and Install:**
   o Go to Android Studio's official website and download the installer for your operating system.
   o Run the installer and follow the on-screen instructions.
2. **Set Up Android Studio:**
   o Open Android Studio after installation and select the **Standard installation** option. This installs all necessary components like the Android SDK, Android Emulator, etc.

3. **Install Flutter and Dart Plugins:**
   - Once Android Studio is installed, open it and go to **Preferences > Plugins**.
   - Search for **Flutter** and **Dart**, and install both plugins to enable Flutter support within Android Studio.

Installing Xcode (macOS only):

- If you are developing for iOS, you need Xcode installed. You can download it from the **Mac App Store**.
- After installation, ensure that the Xcode command-line tools are set up correctly:

```bash
sudo xcode-select --install
```

Configuring Your First Flutter Project

Now that you've installed Flutter, Android Studio, and Xcode (for macOS users), it's time to configure your first Flutter project.

1. **Create a New Flutter Project:**
   - Open Android Studio and select **Start a New Flutter Project**.
   - Choose **Flutter Application** and click **Next**.

30

o Enter the project name (e.g., `my_first_flutter_app`), the location where you want to save the project, and the description.

o Select the appropriate Flutter SDK path (Android Studio should auto-detect it).

2. **Project Structure:**

o After the project is created, you'll see the following folder structure:

- `lib/`: Contains the main Dart code for your app.

- `ios/`: Contains iOS-specific project files.

- `android/`: Contains Android-specific project files.

- `pubspec.yaml`: A file where you specify dependencies and project settings.

3. **Run Your First Flutter App:**

o Open the `lib/main.dart` file. This file contains the entry point for your app.

o The default template will display a counter app. To run it, click on the **Run** button (a green triangle) in Android Studio.

o Select an emulator or a connected device to run the app.

31

Understanding the Flutter CLI and IDEs

Flutter supports both a **Command-Line Interface (CLI)** and **Integrated Development Environments (IDEs)**.

Flutter CLI:

- The Flutter CLI allows developers to interact with Flutter projects via commands in the terminal.
    - `flutter create <project_name>`: Creates a new Flutter project.
    - `flutter run`: Runs the app on the connected device or emulator.
    - `flutter build apk`: Builds the APK for Android.
    - `flutter doctor`: Checks your development environment for issues.

Flutter IDEs:

- **Android Studio**: The primary IDE for Flutter development, with excellent Flutter and Dart plugin support.
- **Visual Studio Code**: A lightweight IDE with Flutter and Dart extensions, suitable for developers who prefer minimal setups.

Running Your First Flutter App

1. **Open Your Project:**
   o   Open the project you created earlier in Android Studio or your preferred IDE.

2. **Configure an Emulator:**
   o   In Android Studio, open the **AVD Manager** (Android Virtual Device), create a virtual device (emulator), and start it.

3. **Run the App:**
   o   Click the **Run** button in the IDE, select the emulator or device, and watch as your first Flutter app is launched.

4. **Hot Reload:**
   o   Flutter offers the **Hot Reload** feature, which allows you to see the changes in your app instantly. Modify the code, save it, and you'll see the changes applied immediately without restarting the app.

In this chapter, you learned how to install and set up your development environment on Windows, macOS, or Linux. You've also configured your first Flutter project and run your first app. This setup provides the foundation for building beautiful and powerful cross-platform mobile apps with Flutter!

CHAPTER 3

THE FUNDAMENTALS OF DART

In this chapter, we will dive into Dart, the programming language used to build Flutter apps. Dart is an object-oriented, class-based language developed by Google, and it's designed to be both efficient and easy to learn. We'll cover the basics of Dart programming, starting from variables and data types to working with collections and handling errors.

Introduction to Dart Programming Language

Dart is a modern programming language that serves as the backbone for Flutter. It is easy to learn for developers with experience in languages like Java, JavaScript, and C#. Dart provides robust support for both functional and object-oriented programming, making it flexible and efficient for building mobile apps, web apps, and even server-side applications.

Key features of Dart:

- **Statically typed**: Dart has a static type system, which helps catch errors at compile-time.
- **Object-Oriented**: Everything in Dart is an object, including numbers, functions, and even `null`.

- **Just-in-Time (JIT) and Ahead-of-Time (AOT) Compilation**: Dart can compile code at runtime (JIT) for fast development cycles or compile to optimized machine code (AOT) for better performance in production.

- **Asynchronous Programming**: Dart has excellent support for asynchronous programming with `async` and `await` keywords, making it perfect for tasks like network requests or long-running operations.

Variables, Data Types, and Operators in Dart

Variables in Dart

Variables are used to store data that can be used throughout the app. In Dart, you can define a variable using either the `var` keyword or by specifying the type explicitly.

- **Dynamic Variables**:
  - Dart allows dynamic typing with `var`, meaning the variable's type is determined at runtime.

```dart
var name = 'Flutter';  // Type inferred as String
```

- **Explicitly Typed Variables**:
  - You can also explicitly define a variable's type.

36

```
dart

String language = 'Dart';
int year = 2025;
```

Data Types in Dart

Dart provides several built-in data types that allow you to handle various kinds of data.

- **Primitive Types**:
    - int: Integer values, e.g., `int age = 30;`
    - double: Floating-point numbers, e.g., `double pi = 3.14;`
    - String: Text values, e.g., `String greeting = 'Hello, World!';`
    - bool: Boolean values, either `true` or `false`, e.g., `bool isActive = true;`
- **Null**: Dart has a `null` type, which represents a variable that doesn't have a value. You can use `null` explicitly or rely on Dart's null safety feature to avoid null dereference errors.

Operators in Dart

Dart supports common operators like arithmetic, relational, and logical operators.

- **Arithmetic Operators**:

```dart
int sum = 5 + 3;        // Addition
int difference = 5 - 3; // Subtraction
int product = 5 * 3;    // Multiplication
double quotient = 5 / 3; // Division
int remainder = 5 % 3;   // Modulo
```

- **Relational Operators**:

```dart
bool isEqual = 5 == 3;  // False
bool isGreaterThan = 5 > 3; // True
```

- **Logical Operators**:

```dart
bool and = true && false;  // False
bool or = true || false;   // True
bool not = !true;          // False
```

Functions, Classes, and Objects

Functions in Dart

Functions in Dart are defined using the void keyword (if the function doesn't return anything) or the return type of the function. A function can take parameters and return a value.

38

- **Function Definition**:

dart

```
int add(int a, int b) {
   return a + b;
}
```

- **Function Call**:

dart

```
int result = add(5, 3); // Calls the add
function
```

- **Arrow Syntax for Short Functions**: For simple functions, Dart allows a shorthand syntax using =>.

dart

```
int multiply(int a, int b) => a * b;
```

Classes in Dart

Dart is an object-oriented language, and you can define classes to create objects.

- **Class Definition**:

dart

```
class Person {
  String name;
  int age;

  // Constructor
  Person(this.name, this.age);

  // Method
  void introduce() {
    print('Hi, I am $name and I am $age
years old.');
  }
}
```

- **Creating an Object**:

dart

```
Person person = Person('Alice', 30);
person.introduce();  // Outputs: Hi, I am
Alice and I am 30 years old.
```

Objects in Dart

Objects are instances of classes. In Dart, all data, including numbers and functions, are objects.

- **Accessing Properties and Methods**:

dart

40

```
print(person.name); // Alice
person.introduce(); // Calling the method
```

Working with Collections (Lists, Maps, Sets)

Lists:

Lists in Dart are ordered collections of items. They are similar to arrays in other languages.

- **Creating a List**:

```dart
List<String> names = ['Alice', 'Bob', 'Charlie'];
```

- **Accessing List Items**:

```dart
print(names[0]); // Alice
```

- **Adding/Removing Items**:

```dart
names.add('David'); // Adds 'David' to the list
```

41

```
names.removeAt(1);   // Removes the item at
index 1 (Bob)
```

Maps:

Maps are key-value pairs, similar to dictionaries in Python or hashmaps in Java.

- **Creating a Map**:

  dart

  ```
  Map<String, int> ages = {'Alice': 30,
  'Bob': 25};
  ```

- **Accessing Values**:

  dart

  ```
  print(ages['Alice']);   // 30
  ```

- **Adding/Removing Key-Value Pairs**:

  dart

  ```
  ages['Charlie'] = 35;   // Adds a new key-
  value pair
  ages.remove('Bob');   // Removes the key
  'Bob' from the map
  ```

Sets:

Sets in Dart are unordered collections of unique items.

- **Creating a Set**:

dart

```
Set<int> numbers = {1, 2, 3};
```

- **Adding/Removing Items**:

dart

```
numbers.add(4);  // Adds 4 to the set
numbers.remove(2); // Removes 2 from the set
```

Error Handling in Dart

Dart provides robust error handling mechanisms using `try`, `catch`, and `finally` blocks. Proper error handling helps in creating apps that are resilient and provide better user experience.

Try-Catch Block:

dart

```
try {
```

```
  int result = 10 ~/ 0;  // Integer division by
zero
} catch (e) {
  print('Error occurred: $e');
}
```

Finally Block:

The `finally` block is used to execute code that must run whether an exception is thrown or not.

dart

```
try {
  // Some code that may throw an exception
} catch (e) {
  // Handle the exception
} finally {
  print('This will always run.');
}
```

Custom Exceptions:

You can define your own exceptions using classes.

dart

```
class MyCustomException implements Exception {
  String errorMessage() => 'Something went
wrong!';
}
```

```
void throwException() {
  throw MyCustomException();
}

try {
  throwException();
} catch (e) {
  print(e.errorMessage());
}
```

In this chapter, we covered the foundational aspects of Dart, including its variables, data types, functions, classes, and objects. You also learned how to work with collections like Lists, Maps, and Sets, and handle errors effectively using Dart's built-in error handling mechanisms. Understanding these fundamentals will enable you to start writing effective and maintainable Dart code, setting the stage for building sophisticated Flutter apps in the next chapters.

CHAPTER 4

FLUTTER WIDGETS – THE BUILDING BLOCKS

In Flutter, everything is a widget. Whether it's a simple button, an image, a complex layout, or a full screen, it's all part of the widget tree. Understanding how Flutter widgets work is key to building effective and responsive user interfaces for your mobile apps. This chapter covers the basics of Flutter widgets, including the widget tree, stateless vs. stateful widgets, and several essential widgets for building your app's UI.

Understanding Flutter's Widget Tree

At the core of every Flutter application is the **widget tree**, a hierarchical structure that defines the UI of your app. A widget represents a part of the UI, and it can be a visual element, such as a button, text, or an image, or an invisible element like padding or alignment.

- **Widget Tree Structure**:
    - The widget tree is a tree of widgets that the Flutter framework uses to render the app's UI.

o   Each widget is a node in the tree, and widgets can have child widgets, forming a parent-child relationship.

o   The root of the tree is typically the **MaterialApp** widget, which is the entry point for your Flutter app.

o   As the widget tree grows, Flutter optimizes rendering by only updating parts of the UI that have changed.

For example:

dart

```
MaterialApp(
  home: Scaffold(
    appBar: AppBar(title: Text('My  Flutter
App')),
    body:      Center(child:      Text('Hello,
Flutter!')),
  ),
);
```

In this example:

- MaterialApp is the root widget.
- Scaffold is a child widget of MaterialApp.

- AppBar and Center are children of Scaffold, and so on.

Stateless vs. Stateful Widgets

In Flutter, widgets fall into two categories: **Stateless widgets** and **Stateful widgets**. The main difference between them lies in whether or not the widget's state can change during the app's lifecycle.

Stateless Widgets

- **Definition**: A stateless widget is a widget that does not depend on any mutable state. Once it's built, it doesn't change over time unless the parent widget changes it.
- **Use Case**: Use stateless widgets when the widget's appearance is static and doesn't require updates after it's first built.

Example:

```dart

class MyStatelessWidget extends StatelessWidget {
  @override
  Widget build(BuildContext context) {
```

```
    return Text('This is a Stateless Widget');
  }
}
```

In this example, the text doesn't change dynamically once the widget is created.

Stateful Widgets

- **Definition**: A stateful widget is a widget that has a mutable state. The widget can rebuild itself when its state changes, making it ideal for interactive UIs.
- **Use Case**: Use stateful widgets for dynamic content, such as form inputs, counters, and any UI that requires changes during its lifecycle.

Example:

dart

```
class CounterWidget extends StatefulWidget {
  @override
  _CounterWidgetState      createState()        =>
_CounterWidgetState();
}

class        _CounterWidgetState           extends
State<CounterWidget> {
  int _counter = 0;
```

```
void _incrementCounter() {
  setState(() {
    _counter++;
  });
}


@override
Widget build(BuildContext context) {
  return Column(
    mainAxisAlignment:
MainAxisAlignment.center,
    children: [
      Text('Counter: $_counter'),
      ElevatedButton(
        onPressed: _incrementCounter,
        child: Text('Increment'),
      ),
    ],
  );
}
}
```

Here, the CounterWidget is a stateful widget because it holds a mutable state (_counter) that changes when the user presses the button.

Basic Widgets: Text, Image, Column, Row, Container

Flutter provides several **basic widgets** that are essential for creating user interfaces. Let's explore the most commonly used ones:

Text Widget

The Text widget is used to display a string of text in your app.

Example:

```dart
dart
```

```dart
Text('Hello, Flutter!')
```

Image Widget

The Image widget is used to display images in your app. It can load images from assets, network URLs, or files.

Example:

```dart
dart
```

```dart
Image.asset('assets/images/flutter_logo.png') // Local asset image
```

or

dart

```
Image.network('https://example.com/flutter_logo
.png') // Network image
```

Column Widget

The Column widget is a layout widget that arranges its children vertically.

Example:

dart

```
Column(
  children: [
    Text('First Item'),
    Text('Second Item'),
    Text('Third Item'),
  ],
)
```

Row Widget

The Row widget is similar to Column but arranges its children horizontally.

Example:

dart

```
Row (
    children:  [
        Icon(Icons.home),
        Text('Home'),
        Icon(Icons.settings),
    ],
)
```

Container Widget

The Container widget is a versatile and powerful widget used for combining other widgets with properties like padding, margin, decoration, and alignment.

Example:

dart

```
Container (
    padding: EdgeInsets.all(10),
    margin: EdgeInsets.symmetric(vertical: 20),
    color: Colors.blue,
    child: Text('This is inside a container'),
)
```

Layout Widgets: Stack, ListView, GridView

Layout widgets in Flutter are used to control how the children of a widget are arranged. These layout widgets help create complex and responsive designs.

Stack Widget

The Stack widget allows you to layer widgets on top of each other. This is useful for creating complex designs where widgets overlap.

Example:

dart

```
Stack(
  children: [

Image.asset('assets/images/background.png'),
    Positioned(
      left: 20,
      top: 30,
      child:    Text('Overlay    Text',    style:
TextStyle(color: Colors.white)),
    ),
  ],
)
```

ListView Widget

The `ListView` widget is used to display a scrolling list of widgets. It can handle a large number of items efficiently by only building the widgets that are currently visible.

Example:

dart

```
ListView(
  children: [
    ListTile(title: Text('Item 1')),
    ListTile(title: Text('Item 2')),
    ListTile(title: Text('Item 3')),
  ],
)
```

GridView Widget

The `GridView` widget is used to display a grid of widgets, ideal for displaying images, products, or any content that can be organized into rows and columns.

Example:

dart

```
GridView.count(
  crossAxisCount: 2, // Two columns
```

```
children: List.generate(6, (index) {
  return Card(
    child: Center(child: Text('Item $index')),
  );
}),
)
```

Real-world Examples Using Basic Widgets

To solidify your understanding of Flutter's basic widgets, let's look at a real-world example. Imagine you are building a simple **profile page** with an image, name, and a list of interests.

dart

```
class ProfilePage extends StatelessWidget {
  @override
  Widget build(BuildContext context) {
    return Scaffold(
      appBar: AppBar(title: Text('Profile')),
      body: Padding(
        padding: const EdgeInsets.all(16.0),
        child: Column(
          children: [
            // Profile Image
            CircleAvatar(
              radius: 50,
```

```
            backgroundImage:
NetworkImage('https://example.com/profile.jpg')
,
            ),
            SizedBox(height: 10),
            // Name
            Text('John        Doe',        style:
TextStyle(fontSize:      24,       fontWeight:
FontWeight.bold)),
            SizedBox(height: 10),
            // Interests List
            Text('Interests:'),
            ListView(
              shrinkWrap: true,
              children: [
                ListTile(title: Text('Coding')),
                ListTile(title:
Text('Reading')),
                ListTile(title: Text('Gaming')),
              ],
            ),
          ],
        ),
      ),
    );
  }
}
```

In this example:

- A `CircleAvatar` is used to display the profile picture.
- `Text` widgets are used to display the name and interests.
- `ListView` is used to create a scrollable list of interests.

Summary

In this chapter, we covered the essentials of Flutter widgets. You learned about:

- **The widget tree** that drives the UI in Flutter.
- **Stateless and stateful widgets** and when to use each type.
- **Basic widgets** like `Text`, `Image`, `Column`, `Row`, and `Container` that help you build a UI.
- **Layout widgets** such as `Stack`, `ListView`, and `GridView` that allow you to design complex, responsive UIs.
- A **real-world example** that brings everything together in a simple profile page.

These building blocks are foundational for creating dynamic, beautiful apps in Flutter. As you progress, you'll dive deeper into more complex widgets and layout techniques.

CHAPTER 5

FLUTTER UI DESIGN –
BUILDING BEAUTIFUL
INTERFACES

Flutter's ability to create beautiful, responsive user interfaces is one of its strongest features. In this chapter, we'll explore the design principles that make Flutter apps both visually appealing and functional. We'll cover **Material Design**, **Cupertino widgets**, customizing widgets to create unique UIs, and designing responsive layouts. By the end of this chapter, you will be able to create stunning user interfaces for both Android and iOS with ease.

Material Design Principles in Flutter

Material Design is a design language developed by Google, and it is widely used for building intuitive, aesthetically pleasing, and consistent UIs. Flutter comes with a rich set of widgets that follow Material Design principles, making it easier for developers to create apps that feel cohesive and visually engaging.

Key Material Design Elements:

- **Layout and Structure**: Material Design encourages the use of cards, lists, and grids to structure content. It emphasizes consistency across the app with a focus on clear, easy navigation.
- **Typography**: Material Design uses specific font sizes and styles for readability. For example, the primary text is usually set in a large, bold style, while secondary text is more subtle.
- **Color Palette**: Material Design uses a set of standard colors (primary, secondary, and background) to ensure that apps are visually balanced.
- **Elevation**: Flutter's `Material` widgets use shadow effects and elevation to create the illusion of depth, helping elements stand out or recede in the UI.

Material Components in Flutter:

- **AppBar**: The AppBar is the top navigation bar in a Flutter app. It typically contains a title, icons, and actions.

Example:

```dart
AppBar(
  title: Text('My Flutter App'),
```

```
  actions: [Icon(Icons.search)],
);
```

- **FloatingActionButton**: This is a circular button that typically performs a primary action in the app.

  Example:

  dart

  ```
  FloatingActionButton(
    onPressed: () {
      // Action goes here
    },
    child: Icon(Icons.add),
  );
  ```

- **Card**: A Material Design card is used to display related information within a container with rounded corners and shadow effects.

  Example:

  dart

  ```
  Card(
    elevation: 5,
    child: ListTile(
      title: Text('Title'),
      subtitle: Text('Subtitle'),
  ```

61

```
    ),
  );
```

Material Design's principles help you design an app that feels intuitive and easy to use, with smooth animations and user-friendly navigation.

Cupertino Widgets for iOS Apps

While Material Design is the go-to design system for Android, **Cupertino widgets** are Flutter's answer for iOS-specific UI elements. Cupertino widgets mimic the design patterns and style of iOS, allowing you to create apps that feel native on iPhones and iPads.

Cupertino Widgets in Flutter:

- **CupertinoNavigationBar**: The iOS-style navigation bar with a back button, title, and actions.

  Example:

  dart

```
CupertinoNavigationBar(
   middle: Text('Cupertino Example'),
   trailing: CupertinoButton(
     child: Icon(CupertinoIcons.add),
```

```
    onPressed: () {},
  ),
);
```

- **CupertinoButton**: The iOS-styled button with no elevation.

  Example:

  dart

```
CupertinoButton(
  child: Text('Click Me'),
  onPressed: () {},
);
```

- **CupertinoAlertDialog**: A dialog widget that is styled according to iOS guidelines.

  Example:

  dart

```
CupertinoAlertDialog(
  title: Text('Alert'),
  content: Text('This is a Cupertino Alert
Dialog'),
  actions: [
    CupertinoDialogAction(
      child: Text('OK'),
```

```
    onPressed: () {
      // Action
    },
  ),
  ],
);
```

When developing apps for both Android and iOS, you can easily switch between Material and Cupertino widgets using conditional logic or by checking the platform with `Platform.isIOS`.

Customizing Widgets to Create Stunning UIs

One of Flutter's greatest strengths is its ability to customize widgets to suit your app's unique design needs. You can adjust various properties of widgets, such as color, padding, margin, shape, and more, to create personalized layouts.

Customizing Widgets:

- **Container**: The `Container` widget is one of the most flexible widgets in Flutter. You can customize it with properties like padding, margin, decoration, and more.

  Example:

  dart

```
Container(
  padding: EdgeInsets.all(20),
  margin: EdgeInsets.all(10),
  decoration: BoxDecoration(
    color: Colors.blue,
    borderRadius:
BorderRadius.circular(10),
  ),
  child: Text('Custom Container'),
);
```

- **Text Styling**: You can customize the Text widget with various properties like fontSize, fontWeight, color, and letterSpacing.

  Example:

  dart

```
Text(
  'Stylish Text',
  style: TextStyle(
    fontSize: 24,
    fontWeight: FontWeight.bold,
    color: Colors.purple,
  ),
);
```

- **Custom Buttons**: You can also create custom buttons by combining `Container` and `GestureDetector` or using `InkWell` to add a ripple effect.

Example:

```dart
GestureDetector(
  onTap: () {
    print('Button pressed');
  },
  child: Container(
    padding:
EdgeInsets.symmetric(vertical:          12,
horizontal: 24),
    decoration: BoxDecoration(
      color: Colors.green,
      borderRadius:
BorderRadius.circular(8),
    ),
    child: Text(
      'Custom Button',
      style:                 TextStyle(color:
Colors.white),
    ),
  ),
);
```

Customizing widgets allows you to design unique UIs, giving your app a distinct look and feel.

Responsive Design with Flutter

With so many different screen sizes and resolutions in the world, building responsive UIs is essential. Flutter makes it easy to create layouts that adjust to different screen sizes and orientations.

Responsive Layout Techniques:

- **MediaQuery**: MediaQuery provides information about the screen size, orientation, and other properties of the device's display.

  Example:

  dart

  ```
  double          screenWidth          =
  MediaQuery.of(context).size.width;
  double          screenHeight          =
  MediaQuery.of(context).size.height;

  if (screenWidth < 600) {
    // Phone layout
  } else {
    // Tablet or large screen layout
  ```

67

```
}
```

- **LayoutBuilder**: LayoutBuilder allows you to build layouts based on the parent widget's constraints, making it perfect for responsive designs.

Example:

dart

```
LayoutBuilder(
    builder: (context, constraints) {
        if (constraints.maxWidth < 600) {
            return              Column(children:
[Text('Mobile View')]);
        } else {
            return  Row(children:  [Text('Tablet
View')]);
        }
    },
);
```

- **Flexible and Expanded**: These widgets help in making widgets flexible within a layout. Flexible allows a widget to adapt to available space, and Expanded forces a widget to take up remaining space.

Example:

```dart
dart
```

```dart
Row(
  children: [
    Expanded(child:    Container(color:
Colors.blue)),
    Expanded(child:    Container(color:
Colors.red)),
  ],
);
```

By using these responsive design techniques, your app will be able to adjust to different screen sizes, ensuring a great user experience on any device.

Example: Building a Simple Login Page

Let's bring everything together and build a simple login page that is styled with Material Design principles, has custom widgets, and is responsive.

```dart
dart
```

```dart
class LoginPage extends StatelessWidget {
  @override
  Widget build(BuildContext context) {
    return Scaffold(
      appBar: AppBar(title: Text('Login')),
```

```
body: Padding(
  padding: EdgeInsets.all(20),
  child: Column(
    mainAxisAlignment:
MainAxisAlignment.center,
    children: [
      Text(
        'Welcome Back!',
        style:   TextStyle(fontSize:   24,
fontWeight: FontWeight.bold),
      ),
      SizedBox(height: 40),
      TextField(
        decoration: InputDecoration(
          labelText: 'Username',
          border: OutlineInputBorder(),
        ),
      ),
      SizedBox(height: 20),
      TextField(
        decoration: InputDecoration(
          labelText: 'Password',
          border: OutlineInputBorder(),
        ),
        obscureText: true,
      ),
      SizedBox(height: 40),
      ElevatedButton(
        onPressed: () {
```

```
                    // Login action
              },
              child: Text('Log In'),
              style: ElevatedButton.styleFrom(
                padding:
EdgeInsets.symmetric(vertical: 15),
                    minimumSize:
Size(double.infinity, 50),
                ),
              ),
          ],
        ),
      ),
    );
  }
}
```

In this example:

- We use `TextField` widgets to collect the username and password from the user.
- The `ElevatedButton` is styled to look visually appealing with a large tap area for easy interaction.
- The UI adjusts dynamically to different screen sizes by utilizing the `SizedBox` for spacing.

Summary

In this chapter, we explored the following key topics:

- **Material Design**: We learned how to use Material Design widgets to build intuitive and aesthetically pleasing UIs.
- **Cupertino Widgets**: We discovered how to use iOS-specific widgets to create apps that feel native to Apple devices.
- **Customizing Widgets**: We explored how to personalize widgets to meet the unique design needs of your app.
- **Responsive Design**: We learned techniques to create flexible layouts that adapt to different screen sizes and orientations.
- **Real-World Example**: We built a simple login page to demonstrate how to put all these concepts into practice.

By mastering these concepts, you'll be well on your way to creating beautiful, responsive, and user-friendly Flutter apps.

CHAPTER 6

NAVIGATING BETWEEN SCREENS

In this chapter, we will explore how to navigate between different screens in a Flutter app. Navigating between screens (also called **routes**) is a fundamental aspect of app development, as it allows you to create a fluid user experience with multiple pages or sections. We will cover how to use the `Navigator` widget for screen transitions, how to pass data between screens, and how to use **named routes** for better organization and management of navigation.

Using Navigator for Screen Transitions

In Flutter, screen navigation is handled by the `Navigator` widget. The `Navigator` is responsible for managing a stack of screens (routes) and allows you to push new screens onto the stack or pop them off.

Basic Navigation with Navigator

To navigate to a new screen, you use the `Navigator.push` method. To return to the previous screen, you use `Navigator.pop`.

1. **Navigating to a New Screen:**

    dart

    ```
    Navigator.push(
      context,
      MaterialPageRoute(builder: (context) =>
    NewScreen()),
    );
    ```

    This will push `NewScreen` onto the navigation stack.

2. **Popping the Current Screen:**

    dart

    ```
    Navigator.pop(context);
    ```

    This will pop the current screen off the stack and return to the previous screen.

Example: Basic Navigation

Let's create a simple app with two screens and navigate between them.

dart

```dart
class FirstScreen extends StatelessWidget {
  @override
  Widget build(BuildContext context) {
    return Scaffold(
      appBar:     AppBar(title:     Text('First
Screen')),
      body: Center(
        child: ElevatedButton(
          onPressed: () {
            Navigator.push(
              context,
              MaterialPageRoute(builder:
(context) => SecondScreen()),
            );
          },
          child: Text('Go to Second Screen'),
        ),
      ),
    );
  }
}
```

```
class SecondScreen extends StatelessWidget {
  @override
  Widget build(BuildContext context) {
    return Scaffold(
      appBar:    AppBar(title:    Text('Second
Screen')),
      body: Center(
        child: ElevatedButton(
          onPressed: () {
            Navigator.pop(context);
          },
          child: Text('Back to First Screen'),
        ),
      ),
    );
  }
}
```

In this example:

- On the **First Screen**, when the user presses the button, the app navigates to the **Second Screen**.
- On the **Second Screen**, when the user presses the button, the app pops the screen off the stack and returns to the **First Screen**.

Passing Data Between Screens

Often, when navigating between screens, you need to pass data from one screen to another. Flutter makes this easy with the `Navigator.push` method, where you can pass data as part of the route.

Passing Data with Constructor Parameters

To pass data, simply define a constructor for the destination screen and send data when navigating.

Example:

```dart
dart

class DetailScreen extends StatelessWidget {
  final String itemName;

  // Constructor to receive data
  DetailScreen({required this.itemName});

  @override
  Widget build(BuildContext context) {
    return Scaffold(
      appBar: AppBar(title: Text(itemName)),
      body: Center(
        child: Text('You selected $itemName'),
      ),
```

```
    );
  }
}


class HomeScreen extends StatelessWidget {
  @override
  Widget build(BuildContext context) {
    return Scaffold(
      appBar:    AppBar(title:    Text('Home
Screen')),
      body: Center(
        child: ElevatedButton(
          onPressed: () {
            Navigator.push(
              context,
              MaterialPageRoute(
                builder:    (context)    =>
DetailScreen(itemName: 'Item 1'),
              ),
            );
          },
          child: Text('Go to Details'),
        ),
      ),
    );
  }
}
```

In this example:

- The `DetailScreen` receives the `itemName` as a constructor parameter.
- When navigating from `HomeScreen`, we pass the string `'Item 1'` to `DetailScreen`.

Using Arguments with Navigator.pushNamed

Another way to pass data is through **named routes**. Named routes allow you to define the route names in one place, making navigation more organized, especially for large apps.

Named Routes in Flutter

Named routes in Flutter help organize navigation, especially in apps with many screens. Instead of passing widgets directly through `MaterialPageRoute`, you define named routes in a `Route` table (in `MaterialApp`) and refer to these routes by name.

Defining Named Routes

To define named routes, you'll use the `routes` property of the `MaterialApp` widget.

Example:

```dart
```

```dart
void main() {
  runApp(MyApp());
}


class MyApp extends StatelessWidget {
  @override
  Widget build(BuildContext context) {
    return MaterialApp(
      initialRoute: '/',
      routes: {
        '/': (context) => HomeScreen(),
        '/details': (context) => DetailScreen(),
      },
    );
  }
}


class HomeScreen extends StatelessWidget {
  @override
  Widget build(BuildContext context) {
    return Scaffold(
      appBar:      AppBar(title:      Text('Home
Screen')),
      body: Center(
        child: ElevatedButton(
          onPressed: () {
            Navigator.pushNamed(context,
'/details');
          },
```

```
            child: Text('Go to Details Screen'),
          ),
        ),
      );
  }
}


class DetailScreen extends StatelessWidget {
  @override
  Widget build(BuildContext context) {
    return Scaffold(
      appBar:    AppBar(title:    Text('Detail
Screen')),
      body: Center(
        child: Text('This is the Detail Screen'),
      ),
    );
  }
}
```

In this example:

- We define the named routes `HomeScreen` and `DetailScreen` in the `routes` property.
- Navigation between the screens is done via `Navigator.pushNamed`, which uses the route name (`/details`) to navigate.

Passing Data with Named Routes

You can also pass data when navigating with named routes. This can be done by using the `arguments` property in the `Navigator.pushNamed` method and accessing it in the destination screen.

Example:

```dart
Navigator.pushNamed(
  context,
  '/details',
  arguments: 'Item 1',
);

class DetailScreen extends StatelessWidget {
  @override
  Widget build(BuildContext context) {
    final String itemName =
ModalRoute.of(context)!.settings.arguments as
String;

    return Scaffold(
      appBar: AppBar(title: Text(itemName)),
      body: Center(
        child: Text('You selected $itemName'),
      ),
```

```
    );
  }
}
```

Here:

- Data (`'Item 1'`) is passed using `arguments`.
- In `DetailScreen`, we retrieve the data using `ModalRoute.of(context)!.settings.argument`
  `s`.

Real-World Example: Building a Simple Shopping App with Multiple Screens

Let's build a simple shopping app that has two screens: a **Product List** screen and a **Product Detail** screen. We'll pass data (the selected product) between these screens and use named routes for navigation.

Step 1: Define the Routes

dart

```
void main() {
  runApp(MyApp());
}

class MyApp extends StatelessWidget {
  @override
```

```dart
Widget build(BuildContext context) {
  return MaterialApp(
    initialRoute: '/',
    routes: {
      '/': (context) => ProductListScreen(),
      '/details':          (context)              =>
ProductDetailScreen(),
    },
  );
}
}
```

Step 2: Create the Product List Screen

dart

```dart
class ProductListScreen extends StatelessWidget
{
  final  List<String>  products  =  ['Laptop',
'Phone', 'Tablet'];

  @override
  Widget build(BuildContext context) {
    return Scaffold(
      appBar:   AppBar(title:    Text('Product
List')),
      body: ListView.builder(
        itemCount: products.length,
        itemBuilder: (context, index) {
          return ListTile(
            title: Text(products[index]),
```

84

```
          onTap: () {
            Navigator.pushNamed(
              context,
              '/details',
              arguments: products[index],
            );
          },
        );
      },
    ),
  );
  }
}
```

Step 3: Create the Product Detail Screen

dart

```
class        ProductDetailScreen        extends
StatelessWidget {
  @override
  Widget build(BuildContext context) {
    final        String        productName        =
ModalRoute.of(context)!.settings.arguments        as
String;

    return Scaffold(
      appBar:     AppBar(title:     Text('Product
Details')),
      body: Center(
        child: Text('Details of $productName'),
```

```
            ),
        );
    }
}
```

Step 4: Run the App

- The **Product List Screen** displays a list of products. When a product is tapped, it navigates to the **Product Detail Screen** and passes the product name.

- The **Product Detail Screen** displays the product name, which is passed from the previous screen.

Summary

In this chapter, we explored:

- **Using the Navigator** widget to navigate between screens and manage the app's route stack.

- **Passing data between screens** using constructor parameters and the `arguments` property with named routes.

- **Named routes** for better route management and organization in large apps.

- A **real-world example** of building a simple shopping app with multiple screens that interact with each other.

By mastering these navigation concepts, you can create seamless user experiences in Flutter, making your app feel intuitive and easy to use.

CHAPTER 7

MANAGING STATE IN FLUTTER

State management is a critical concept in Flutter and any other mobile development framework. It allows your app to maintain and update its data over time. In this chapter, we will dive into **state management** in Flutter, exploring why it's essential for building dynamic, interactive apps. We'll discuss the types of state management, introduce popular state management solutions like **Provider**, **Riverpod**, and **Bloc**, and end with a hands-on example of building a simple counter app using **Provider**.

What is State Management in Flutter?

In Flutter, **state** refers to the data or properties that determine how the UI of an app looks and behaves. State can be anything from user input, like text entered into a form, to data fetched from a network. State management is the process of managing this data, ensuring that the app can update its UI based on changes to the state.

State management is essential in Flutter because Flutter's UI framework is **declarative**, meaning the UI is rebuilt whenever the state changes. This is different from imperative programming, where the developer explicitly tells the system how to update the UI. In Flutter, you define the UI in terms of the state, and the framework takes care of updating the UI when that state changes.

The Importance of State in Mobile Apps

State is central to the functionality and interactivity of any mobile app. Without managing state, an app would have a static UI that doesn't respond to user actions or external events. Here are some examples of where state is essential in mobile apps:

- **User Input**: When a user enters information into a form, the app needs to manage the state of that data (e.g., username, email, password) until it is submitted.
- **Dynamic Data**: Apps often fetch data from APIs, such as weather data or product lists. The app needs to update its UI when new data is available.
- **UI Changes**: Elements like buttons, switches, or checkboxes often change state based on user interaction. For instance, toggling a switch on or off is a state change.

Effectively managing state ensures that the app responds to user interactions and changes in the environment seamlessly, providing a smooth experience.

Local vs Global State

When managing state, it's essential to differentiate between **local state** and **global state**.

Local State:

Local state is used for managing the state of individual widgets, and it's often confined to a specific screen or part of the UI. Local state can be as simple as a counter variable or user input within a form.

- **Example of Local State**: A button that increases the count when pressed.
- **Where to Use Local State**: For small-scale state management that does not need to be shared between multiple widgets or screens.

Local state in Flutter is often managed within a `StatefulWidget` and is updated through the `setState` method.

Global State:

Global state is state that needs to be shared across different parts of the app, often between multiple screens or widgets. For example, if your app has a shopping cart, the cart's items are likely to be used on multiple screens (e.g., product detail and checkout).

- **Example of Global State**: User authentication status, global theme settings, or a shopping cart with items.
- **Where to Use Global State**: When the state needs to be accessed by different widgets or screens, and it should persist throughout the app.

Managing global state efficiently is crucial to avoid performance issues and unnecessary complexity.

Introduction to State Management Solutions (Provider, Riverpod, Bloc, etc.)

Flutter provides several ways to manage state. While **setState** is sufficient for local state management, when dealing with more complex state or global state, you'll need a more robust solution. Here are some of the most popular state management solutions in Flutter:

1. Provider

- **Overview**: Provider is one of the most popular state management solutions in Flutter. It allows you to manage global state and pass data through the widget tree efficiently.
- **Key Features**: Easy to learn, integrates well with Flutter's existing widget tree, and is highly flexible.

- **Use Case**: Ideal for managing simple to moderately complex global state.

2. Riverpod

- **Overview**: Riverpod is a newer state management solution created by the same author as Provider. It aims to improve upon Provider by adding more features, such as better handling of immutable state and easier testing.
- **Key Features**: Enhanced flexibility, built-in support for async data, and a better way to handle lifecycle management.
- **Use Case**: Suitable for apps that require more advanced state management and testing capabilities.

3. Bloc (Business Logic Component)

- **Overview**: Bloc is a more structured state management approach that uses Streams and Sinks to manage state. It is based on the reactive programming paradigm and is ideal for large apps that require a clear separation of business logic and UI.
- **Key Features**: Powerful for complex state management, follows a pattern of handling business logic in separate layers, and can be more verbose than Provider or Riverpod.

- **Use Case**: Best for large-scale apps that require significant business logic and need separation of concerns.

4. Other Solutions

- **Redux**: A more complex solution often used in larger apps that have global state management.
- **Scoped Model**: A simpler approach that works for basic state management but is less flexible than Provider or Riverpod.

Example: Building a Counter App Using Provider

Let's build a simple **counter app** that demonstrates how to use **Provider** for state management. In this app, we will have a counter that can be incremented and decremented using buttons. The state of the counter will be managed globally using `Provider`.

Step 1: Add Provider to `pubspec.yaml`

First, you need to add the `provider` package to your `pubspec.yaml` file:

`yaml`

```
dependencies:
  flutter:
    sdk: flutter
  provider: ^6.0.0 # Make sure to use the latest
version
```

Step 2: Create a Counter Model

We will create a simple `Counter` class that will hold our counter value and provide methods to increment and decrement it.

```dart
import 'package:flutter/material.dart';

class Counter with ChangeNotifier {
  int _count = 0;

  int get count => _count;

  void increment() {
    _count++;
    notifyListeners();  // Notifies all listeners
when the state changes
  }

  void decrement() {
    _count--;
    notifyListeners();
  }
```

```
}
```

Step 3: Set Up Provider in the App

We will use `ChangeNotifierProvider` to provide the `Counter` model to the widget tree.

dart

```
import 'package:flutter/material.dart';
import 'package:provider/provider.dart';
import 'counter.dart';   // Import the Counter
class

void main() {
  runApp(MyApp());
}

class MyApp extends StatelessWidget {
  @override
  Widget build(BuildContext context) {
    return ChangeNotifierProvider(
      create: (context) => Counter(),
      child: MaterialApp(
        title: 'Flutter Counter App',
        home: CounterScreen(),
      ),
    );
  }
}
```

Step 4: Create the Counter Screen

Now, let's build the UI for the counter screen. The CounterScreen will listen for changes to the counter and update the UI accordingly.

dart

```dart
class CounterScreen extends StatelessWidget {
  @override
  Widget build(BuildContext context) {
    return Scaffold(
      appBar:     AppBar(title:     Text('Counter
App')),
      body: Center(
        child: Column(
          mainAxisAlignment:
MainAxisAlignment.center,
          children: [
            // Display the current counter value
            Consumer<Counter>(
              builder: (context, counter, child)
{
                return Text(
                  'Counter: ${counter.count}',
                  style:     TextStyle(fontSize:
30),
                );
              },
```

```
        ),
        SizedBox(height: 20),
        // Increment button
        ElevatedButton(
          onPressed: () {

context.read<Counter>().increment();
          },
          child: Text('Increment'),
        ),
        SizedBox(height: 20),
        // Decrement button
        ElevatedButton(
          onPressed: () {

context.read<Counter>().decrement();
          },
          child: Text('Decrement'),
        ),
      ],
    ),
  ),
);
  }
}
```

Explanation of the Code:

- **ChangeNotifierProvider**: We wrap our app with `ChangeNotifierProvider`, which will manage the state for the `Counter` model.
- **Consumer**: This widget listens to the `Counter` model and rebuilds whenever the state changes (i.e., when the counter value is incremented or decremented).
- **context.read<Counter>()**: We use `context.read` to access the `Counter` model and call its methods to update the state.

Summary

In this chapter, we learned:

- **State management** is crucial for building dynamic and interactive apps. It ensures that data can flow between the UI and backend without issues.
- **Local vs. global state**: Local state is confined to a single widget, while global state is shared across different widgets and screens.
- We explored popular **state management solutions** in Flutter, including **Provider**, **Riverpod**, and **Bloc**, each offering a different approach to managing state.

- We built a simple **counter app** using **Provider**, which demonstrated how to manage state globally and reactively update the UI.

By mastering state management, you'll be able to build apps that are efficient, scalable, and responsive to user actions.

CHAPTER 8

NETWORKING AND HTTP REQUESTS

In modern mobile apps, working with data from external sources is a common requirement. Whether it's pulling content from a server, fetching user data, or displaying real-time information, **networking** and making **HTTP requests** are essential skills for Flutter developers. In this chapter, we'll explore how to work with APIs in Flutter, fetch data using HTTP requests, parse JSON responses, handle errors, and create a real-world weather app that fetches data from an API.

How to Work with APIs in Flutter

An **API (Application Programming Interface)** is a set of rules that allows one piece of software to communicate with another. In Flutter, you can interact with APIs using HTTP requests to fetch data from remote servers. APIs commonly send data in **JSON (JavaScript Object Notation)** format, which you can easily parse in Flutter using the `http` package.

Setting Up for Networking in Flutter

To work with APIs in Flutter, you'll need to add the `http` package to your `pubspec.yaml` file:

```yaml
dependencies:
  flutter:
    sdk: flutter
  http: ^0.13.3
```

After adding this dependency, run `flutter pub get` to install the package.

Fetching Data with HTTP Requests

The primary way to fetch data from an API in Flutter is by using the `http` package. This package allows you to make network requests (GET, POST, etc.) and handle the responses.

Making a Simple GET Request

A GET request is used to retrieve data from the server. Here's how you can make a simple GET request:

```dart
```

```
import 'package:http/http.dart' as http;

Future<void> fetchData() async {
  final          response          =          await
http.get(Uri.parse('https://api.example.com/dat
a'));

  if (response.statusCode == 200) {
    print('Data: ${response.body}');
  } else {
    throw Exception('Failed to load data');
  }
}
```

Explanation:

- **http.get**: This method sends a GET request to the specified URL and returns a `Response` object.
- **statusCode**: This checks the status of the HTTP response. A status code of 200 means the request was successful.
- **response.body**: The body of the response, which contains the actual data.

Making a POST Request

Sometimes, you need to send data to an API using a POST request. Here's an example:

dart

102

```
Future<void> sendData() async {
  final response = await http.post(
    Uri.parse('https://api.example.com/data'),
    body: {'key': 'value'},  // Send data as form
fields
  );

  if (response.statusCode == 200) {
    print('Data sent successfully');
  } else {
    throw Exception('Failed to send data');
  }
}
```

In this example, we send data as form fields in the `body` of the POST request.

Parsing JSON in Dart

Most APIs return data in JSON format, and to use this data in your Flutter app, you need to **parse** it into a Dart object. Dart provides the `dart:convert` library, which includes a `jsonDecode()` function to parse JSON data.

Parsing JSON Response

Here's how you can parse a JSON response from an API:

1. First, add `dart:convert` to your import statements:

```dart
dart
```

```dart
import 'dart:convert';
```

2. Next, decode the JSON response:

```dart
dart
```

```dart
import 'package:http/http.dart' as http;
import 'dart:convert';

Future<void> fetchData() async {
  final response = await
http.get(Uri.parse('https://api.example.c
om/data'));

  if (response.statusCode == 200) {
    // Parse the JSON data
    final Map<String, dynamic> data =
jsonDecode(response.body);
    print(data);  // Printing the parsed
data
  } else {
    throw Exception('Failed to load
data');
  }
}
```

3. If the JSON data is nested, you can access the specific fields like so:

dart

```
print(data['key']);  // Access the value of
'key' from the JSON
```

Creating Dart Models from JSON

For more complex data structures, it's common to create Dart classes to model the JSON response. This will make your data easier to work with.

dart

```
class Weather {
  final String description;
  final double temperature;

  Weather({required this.description, required
this.temperature});

  factory Weather.fromJson(Map<String, dynamic>
json) {
    return Weather(
      description: json['description'],
      temperature:
json['temperature'].toDouble(),
    );
```

```
    }
}
```

In this example:

- The `Weather` class models the weather data.
- The `fromJson` factory constructor helps convert JSON into a `Weather` object.

Handling Errors During Network Requests

Network requests can fail for various reasons: no internet connection, server issues, or invalid URLs. Proper error handling is essential to provide a good user experience.

Handling Errors

You can handle errors in Flutter using `try-catch` blocks to catch exceptions.

Example:

dart

```
Future<void> fetchData() async {
    try {
```

```
final          response          =          await
http.get(Uri.parse('https://api.example.com/dat
a'));

    if (response.statusCode == 200) {
      final data = jsonDecode(response.body);
      print(data);
    } else {
      throw Exception('Failed to load data');
    }
  } catch (e) {
    print('Error: $e');
  }
}
```

In this code:

- If the request fails or the status code is not 200, an exception is thrown.
- The `catch` block catches the error, and you can handle it appropriately (e.g., displaying an error message to the user).

Handling Specific Errors

You can handle specific types of errors, such as network issues:

dart

```
import 'package:http/http.dart' as http;

Future<void> fetchData() async {
  try {
    final response = await
http.get(Uri.parse('https://api.example.com/dat
a'));

    if (response.statusCode == 200) {
      final data = jsonDecode(response.body);
      print(data);
    } else {
      throw Exception('Failed to load data');
    }
  } on http.ClientException catch (e) {
    print('Network error: $e');
  } catch (e) {
    print('General error: $e');
  }
}
```

Real-World Example: Creating a Weather App That Fetches Data from an API

Let's build a simple weather app that fetches data from a weather API and displays the weather details.

1. **Create a Weather Model**: First, create a model class for the weather data.

```dart
class Weather {
  final String description;
  final double temperature;

  Weather({required this.description, required this.temperature});

  factory Weather.fromJson(Map<String, dynamic> json) {
    return Weather(
      description: json['weather'][0]['description'],
      temperature: json['main']['temp'].toDouble(),
    );
  }
}
```

2. **Fetching Weather Data**: Use the `http` package to fetch data from an API.

```dart
import 'package:http/http.dart' as http;
import 'dart:convert';
```

109

```dart
Future<Weather> fetchWeather(String city) async
{
  final apiKey = 'YOUR_API_KEY';  // Replace with
your actual API key
  final response = await http.get(

Uri.parse('https://api.openweathermap.org/data/
2.5/weather?q=$city&appid=$apiKey&units=metric'
),
  );

  if (response.statusCode == 200) {
    final   Map<String,   dynamic>   data   =
jsonDecode(response.body);
    return Weather.fromJson(data);
  } else {
    throw  Exception('Failed  to  load  weather
data');
  }
}
```

3. **Displaying the Weather Data**: Now, create the UI to display the weather details.

```dart
dart

import 'package:flutter/material.dart';

class WeatherScreen extends StatelessWidget {
```

110

```dart
  final String city;

  WeatherScreen({required this.city});

  @override
  Widget build(BuildContext context) {
    return Scaffold(
      appBar: AppBar(title: Text('Weather in
$city')),
      body: FutureBuilder<Weather>(
        future: fetchWeather(city),
        builder: (context, snapshot) {
          if (snapshot.connectionState ==
ConnectionState.waiting) {
            return Center(child:
CircularProgressIndicator());
          } else if (snapshot.hasError) {
            return Center(child: Text('Error:
${snapshot.error}'));
          } else if (snapshot.hasData) {
            final weather = snapshot.data!;
            return Padding(
              padding: EdgeInsets.all(16.0),
              child: Column(
                mainAxisAlignment:
MainAxisAlignment.center,
                children: [
```

```
                    Text('Temperature:
${weather.temperature}°C',                    style:
TextStyle(fontSize: 24)),
                       SizedBox(height: 10),
                       Text('Description:
${weather.description}',                    style:
TextStyle(fontSize: 20)),
                    ],
                 ),
               );
            } else {
               return Center(child: Text('No  data
available'));
            }
          },
        ),
      );
   }
}
```

4. **Run the App**: To see the app in action, run it and provide a city name.

dart

```
void main() {
  runApp(MaterialApp(
    home: WeatherScreen(city: 'London'),
  ));
}
```

112

Summary

In this chapter, we covered:

- **Networking** in Flutter using the `http` package to make HTTP requests (GET, POST) to APIs.
- **Parsing JSON** data using `jsonDecode` to convert the JSON response into usable Dart objects.
- **Error handling** during network requests with `try-catch` blocks to ensure smooth user experience.
- A **real-world example** of creating a weather app that fetches data from an API and displays it in the UI.

By mastering these concepts, you'll be able to integrate external data sources into your apps and create dynamic, real-time applications.

CHAPTER 9

LOCAL STORAGE AND DATABASES

In many mobile apps, it's essential to store data locally for offline access, persistence, or caching. Flutter provides several options for local storage, from simple key-value stores to full-fledged relational databases. In this chapter, we will cover how to work with local storage using **SharedPreferences**, how to use **SQLite** in Flutter for more complex data storage, and build a practical example: a **To-Do List App** that uses local storage to save tasks.

Working with Local Storage (SharedPreferences)

SharedPreferences is a simple key-value store that allows you to persist small amounts of data (such as user settings, preferences, or simple flags) locally. It's ideal for saving data that doesn't require the complexity of a database.

Adding SharedPreferences to Your Project

To use SharedPreferences, you need to add the `shared_preferences` package to your `pubspec.yaml` file:

```
yaml
```

```
dependencies:
  flutter:
    sdk: flutter
  shared_preferences: ^2.0.15  # Use the latest
version
```

After adding the dependency, run `flutter pub get` to install it.

Saving and Retrieving Data with SharedPreferences

Here's how you can use SharedPreferences to store and retrieve data:

1. **Saving Data**:

   ```
   dart
   ```

   ```
   import
   'package:shared_preferences/shared_prefer
   ences.dart';

   Future<void> saveData() async {
     final       prefs      =         await
   SharedPreferences.getInstance();
     await         prefs.setString('username',
   'JohnDoe');
     await prefs.setInt('age', 30);
   ```

```
}
```

2. **Retrieving Data**:

dart

```dart
Future<void> loadData() async {
  final prefs = await
SharedPreferences.getInstance();
  String? username =
prefs.getString('username');
  int? age = prefs.getInt('age');

  print('Username: $username, Age: $age');
}
```

3. **Removing Data**:

dart

```dart
Future<void> removeData() async {
  final prefs = await
SharedPreferences.getInstance();
  await prefs.remove('username');
}
```

SharedPreferences is best suited for simple, lightweight storage needs like storing preferences or small data that doesn't require complex querying.

Introduction to SQLite in Flutter

For more complex local storage needs, such as storing structured data with relationships (e.g., tasks, notes, user profiles), **SQLite** is a great option. SQLite is a lightweight, relational database that can be embedded directly into mobile apps.

SQLite allows you to store, retrieve, and manipulate data in tables, which is ideal for use cases like to-do lists, chat apps, and more.

Using the sqflite Plugin

To use SQLite in Flutter, we'll use the `sqflite` plugin. The plugin provides a simple interface for interacting with SQLite databases and helps you perform common database operations like creating tables, inserting records, querying data, and more.

Adding the sqflite Plugin

To get started with SQLite, add the `sqflite` package to your `pubspec.yaml` file:

yaml

```
dependencies:
  flutter:
```

```
sdk: flutter
sqflite: ^2.0.0+3  # Use the latest version
```

After adding the dependency, run `flutter pub get` to install it.

Basic SQLite Operations

1. **Opening a Database**: To interact with the database, you need to open a connection to it.

    ```dart
    dart

    import 'package:sqflite/sqflite.dart';
    import 'package:path/path.dart';

    Future<Database> openDatabase() async {
      final databasePath = await getDatabasesPath();
      final path = join(databasePath, 'todo.db');

      return openDatabase(
        path,
        onCreate: (db, version) {
          return db.execute(
            'CREATE TABLE tasks(id INTEGER PRIMARY KEY, title TEXT, description TEXT)',
          );
    ```

118

```
    },
    version: 1,
  );
}
```

2. **Inserting Data**: To insert data into a table, you can use the `insert` method.

dart

```
Future<void>   insertTask(Database   db,
Map<String, dynamic> task) async {
  await db.insert(
    'tasks',
    task,
    conflictAlgorithm:
ConflictAlgorithm.replace,
  );
}
```

3. **Querying Data**: To retrieve data from the database, use the `query` method.

dart

```
Future<List<Map<String,         dynamic>>>
getTasks(Database db) async {
  return await db.query('tasks');
}
```

119

4. **Updating Data**: You can update existing records using the update method.

dart

```
Future<void> updateTask(Database db, int
id, Map<String, dynamic> updatedTask)
async {
  await db.update(
    'tasks',
    updatedTask,
    where: 'id = ?',
    whereArgs: [id],
  );
}
```

5. **Deleting Data**: To delete records from the database, use the delete method.

dart

```
Future<void> deleteTask(Database db, int
id) async {
  await db.delete(
    'tasks',
    where: 'id = ?',
    whereArgs: [id],
  );
}
```

Example: Building a To-Do List App with Local Storage

Now, let's create a simple **To-Do List app** that uses SQLite for local data storage. The app will allow users to add, display, update, and delete tasks.

Step 1: Define the Task Model

First, we define a simple model to represent a task.

dart

```
class Task {
  final int? id;
  final String title;
  final String description;

  Task({this.id, required this.title, required
this.description});

  Map<String, dynamic> toMap() {
    return {
      'id': id,
      'title': title,
      'description': description,
    };
  }
}
```

```dart
  // Create a Task object from a Map
  factory Task.fromMap(Map<String, dynamic> map)
{
    return Task(
      id: map['id'],
      title: map['title'],
      description: map['description'],
    );
  }
}
```

Step 2: Initialize the Database

We'll create a method to open the database and create the necessary table for tasks.

dart

```dart
Future<Database> initializeDatabase() async {
  final databasePath = await getDatabasesPath();
  final path = join(databasePath, 'tasks.db');
  return openDatabase(
    path,
    onCreate: (db, version) {
      return db.execute(
        'CREATE TABLE tasks(id INTEGER PRIMARY KEY, title TEXT, description TEXT)',
      );
    },
    version: 1,
```

```
    );
}
```

Step 3: Add CRUD Operations

Now, we'll create methods to add, retrieve, update, and delete tasks in the database.

dart

```
Future<void> insertTask(Database db, Task task)
async {
  await db.insert(
    'tasks',
    task.toMap(),
    conflictAlgorithm:
ConflictAlgorithm.replace,
  );
}

Future<List<Task>> getTasks(Database db) async {
  final List<Map<String, dynamic>> maps = await
db.query('tasks');
  return List.generate(maps.length, (i) {
    return Task.fromMap(maps[i]);
  });
}

Future<void> updateTask(Database db, Task task)
async {
```

```dart
await db.update(
  'tasks',
  task.toMap(),
  where: 'id = ?',
  whereArgs: [task.id],
);
}


Future<void> deleteTask(Database db, int id)
async {
  await db.delete(
    'tasks',
    where: 'id = ?',
    whereArgs: [id],
  );
}
```

Step 4: Build the UI

We will create a simple UI to display the tasks and allow the user to add, update, and delete tasks.

dart

```dart
class ToDoListApp extends StatefulWidget {
  @override
  _ToDoListAppState createState() =>
_ToDoListAppState();
}
```

```
class            _ToDoListAppState            extends
State<ToDoListApp> {
  late Database db;
  List<Task> tasks = [];

  @override
  void initState() {
    super.initState();
    initializeDatabase().then((database) {
      db = database;
      loadTasks();
    });
  }

  void loadTasks() async {
    List<Task> loadedTasks = await getTasks(db);
    setState(() {
      tasks = loadedTasks;
    });
  }

  void addTask(String title, String description)
{
    Task   newTask   =   Task(title:   title,
description: description);
    insertTask(db, newTask).then((_) {
      loadTasks();
    });
  }
```

125

```dart
void deleteTask(int id) {
  deleteTask(db, id).then((_) {
    loadTasks();
  });
}

@override
Widget build(BuildContext context) {
  return Scaffold(
    appBar: AppBar(title: Text('To-Do List')),
    body: ListView.builder(
      itemCount: tasks.length,
      itemBuilder: (context, index) {
        Task task = tasks[index];
        return ListTile(
          title: Text(task.title),
          subtitle: Text(task.description),
          trailing: IconButton(
            icon: Icon(Icons.delete),
            onPressed:          ()          =>
deleteTask(task.id!),
          ),
        );
      },
    ),
    floatingActionButton:
FloatingActionButton(
      onPressed: () {
```

```
      // Example of adding a new task
      addTask('New         Task',        'Task
description');
        },
        child: Icon(Icons.add),
      ),
    );
  }
}
```

Step 5: Running the App

Now, when you run the app, you will be able to:

- Add tasks to the database.
- Display tasks in a list.
- Delete tasks from the database.

Summary

In this chapter, we covered:

- **SharedPreferences** for simple key-value storage and how to store and retrieve data.
- **SQLite** for more complex data storage needs, and we used the `sqflite` plugin to interact with an SQLite database.

- **Building a To-Do List app** using SQLite to store tasks locally, which involved defining a task model, setting up the database, and implementing CRUD operations (Create, Read, Update, Delete).

By mastering these concepts, you'll be able to create apps that persist data locally, offering a better user experience with offline access and persistent settings or content.

CHAPTER 10

FLUTTER ANIMATIONS – MAKING APPS COME TO LIFE

In this chapter, we will dive into **animations** in Flutter, a powerful way to make your apps more engaging, dynamic, and interactive. Flutter provides a variety of built-in animation widgets and tools that allow you to animate UI elements with ease. We will cover the different types of animations in Flutter, how to use built-in animation widgets like `AnimatedContainer`, `AnimatedOpacity`, and `TweenAnimationBuilder`, and how to create custom animations. Finally, we will explore a real-world example of adding animations to a **weather app**.

Types of Animations in Flutter (Implicit, Explicit)

Flutter provides two main categories of animations:

1. Implicit Animations

Implicit animations are animations that are automatically handled by Flutter with minimal code. When you change a property of an animated widget (e.g., color, size, position), Flutter automatically animates the change.

- **Examples**: AnimatedContainer, AnimatedOpacity, AnimatedPadding, etc.
- **Usage**: Implicit animations are great for simple UI transitions and visual effects.

2. Explicit Animations

Explicit animations give you more control over the animation process. You can specify the animation duration, curve, and other properties. These animations require you to define an animation controller that controls the animation.

- **Examples**: AnimationController, Tween, AnimatedBuilder.
- **Usage**: Explicit animations are ideal for complex animations where you need fine-grained control over the timing, sequence, and behavior of the animation.

Using AnimatedContainer, AnimatedOpacity, and TweenAnimationBuilder

Flutter offers a range of pre-built animation widgets that make it easy to add animations to your app without writing too much code. Here's how to use some of the most commonly used ones:

1. AnimatedContainer

The `AnimatedContainer` widget is a great choice for animating changes in container properties like size, color, shape, and more.

- **Example**: Animating size and color change with `AnimatedContainer`.

dart

```
class        AnimatedContainerExample        extends
StatefulWidget {
  @override
  _AnimatedContainerExampleState    createState()
=> _AnimatedContainerExampleState();
}

class    _AnimatedContainerExampleState    extends
State<AnimatedContainerExample> {
  double _width = 200;
  double _height = 200;
  Color _color = Colors.blue;

  void _changeProperties() {
    setState(() {
      _width = _width == 200 ? 300 : 200;
      _height = _height == 200 ? 300 : 200;
      _color = _color == Colors.blue ? Colors.red
: Colors.blue;
```

131

```
    });
  }


  @override
  Widget build(BuildContext context) {
    return Scaffold(
      appBar:                          AppBar(title:
Text('AnimatedContainer Example')),
        body: Center(
          child: GestureDetector(
            onTap: _changeProperties,
            child: AnimatedContainer(
              width: _width,
              height: _height,
              color: _color,
              duration: Duration(seconds: 1),
              curve: Curves.easeInOut,
              child:     Center(child:     Text('Tap
me!')),
          ),
        ),
      ),
    );
  }
}
```

In this example:

- The `AnimatedContainer` animates the change of the container's width, height, and color when tapped.
- We define the `duration` and `curve` to control the animation's behavior.

2. AnimatedOpacity

The `AnimatedOpacity` widget animates the opacity of a widget over a given duration. It's useful when you want to fade elements in and out of view.

- **Example**: Fading in and out using `AnimatedOpacity`.

dart

```
class        AnimatedOpacityExample        extends
StatefulWidget {
  @override
  _AnimatedOpacityExampleState createState()  =>
_AnimatedOpacityExampleState();
}

class     _AnimatedOpacityExampleState      extends
State<AnimatedOpacityExample> {
  double _opacity = 1.0;

  void _toggleOpacity() {
    setState(() {
      _opacity = _opacity == 1.0 ? 0.0 : 1.0;
```

```
    });
  }


  @override
  Widget build(BuildContext context) {
    return Scaffold(
      appBar:                         AppBar(title:
Text('AnimatedOpacity Example')),
        body: Center(
          child: GestureDetector(
            onTap: _toggleOpacity,
            child: AnimatedOpacity(
              opacity: _opacity,
              duration: Duration(seconds: 1),
              child: Container(
                width: 200,
                height: 200,
                color: Colors.blue,
                child: Center(child: Text('Tap to
Fade')),
              ),
            ),
          ),
        ),
    );
  }
}
```

Here:

- The `AnimatedOpacity` animates the opacity of the container.
- When tapped, the container fades in and out with a smooth animation.

3. TweenAnimationBuilder

`TweenAnimationBuilder` allows you to animate any property (like size, position, color, etc.) using a `Tween` with a specified duration and curve. It's very versatile and works for both simple and complex animations.

- **Example**: Animating the scale of a widget using `TweenAnimationBuilder`.

dart

```
class     TweenAnimationBuilderExample     extends
StatelessWidget {
  @override
  Widget build(BuildContext context) {
    return Scaffold(
      appBar:                          AppBar(title:
Text('TweenAnimationBuilder Example')),
      body: Center(
        child: TweenAnimationBuilder(
          tween: Tween<double>(begin: 1.0, end:
2.0),
          duration: Duration(seconds: 1),
```

135

```
      builder: (context, scale, child) {
        return Transform.scale(
          scale: scale,
          child: Container(
            width: 200,
            height: 200,
            color: Colors.blue,
            child:                Center(child:
Text('Scaling')),
            ),
          );
        },
      ),
    ),
  );
  }
}
```

In this example:

- The `TweenAnimationBuilder` animates the scale of the widget from 1.0 to 2.0.
- It uses a `Tween` that defines the start and end values for the scale property.

Creating Custom Animations

For more advanced use cases, you may need to create custom animations. Flutter provides powerful tools like AnimationController, Tween, and AnimatedBuilder to create complex, customized animations.

Example: Custom Animation with AnimationController
dart

```dart
class CustomAnimationExample extends StatefulWidget {
  @override
  _CustomAnimationExampleState createState() => _CustomAnimationExampleState();
}

class _CustomAnimationExampleState extends State<CustomAnimationExample> with SingleTickerProviderStateMixin {
  late AnimationController _controller;
  late Animation<double> _animation;

  @override
  void initState() {
    super.initState();

    _controller = AnimationController(
      vsync: this,
```

```
      duration: Duration(seconds: 2),
    );


    _animation = Tween<double>(begin: 0.0, end:
1.0).animate(
        CurvedAnimation(parent:        _controller,
curve: Curves.easeInOut),
      );


    _controller.forward();       //   Start   the
animation
    }


  @override
  void dispose() {
    _controller.dispose();       //   Dispose   the
controller to free resources
    super.dispose();
    }


  @override
  Widget build(BuildContext context) {
    return Scaffold(
      appBar:       AppBar(title:       Text('Custom
Animation Example')),
      body: Center(
        child: FadeTransition(
          opacity: _animation,
          child: Container(
```

```
            width: 200,
            height: 200,
            color: Colors.blue,
            child:    Center(child:    Text('Fading
in!')),
          ),
        ),
      ),
    );
  }
}
```

Explanation:

- We use an `AnimationController` to control the duration and timing of the animation.
- A `Tween` defines the range of values for the animation, and `CurvedAnimation` adds an easing curve to the transition.
- `FadeTransition` is used to apply the opacity animation to the widget.

Example: Adding Animations to a Weather App

Let's combine what we've learned by adding animations to a **weather app** that displays the weather information fetched from an API. The app will include a fade-in animation for the weather details and a smooth transition for changing weather icons.

Step 1: Setup the Basic UI

Create a basic layout to display weather details like temperature, description, and an icon.

dart

```dart
class WeatherApp extends StatelessWidget {
  @override
  Widget build(BuildContext context) {
    return MaterialApp(
      home: WeatherScreen(),
    );
  }
}


class WeatherScreen extends StatefulWidget {
  @override
  _WeatherScreenState createState() =>
_WeatherScreenState();
}


class _WeatherScreenState extends
State<WeatherScreen> with
SingleTickerProviderStateMixin {
  late AnimationController _controller;
```

140

```dart
late Animation<double> _opacityAnimation;

@override
void initState() {
  super.initState();

  _controller = AnimationController(
    vsync: this,
    duration: Duration(seconds: 1),
  );

  _opacityAnimation = Tween<double>(begin:
0.0, end: 1.0).animate(
    CurvedAnimation(parent:      _controller,
curve: Curves.easeInOut),
  );

  _controller.forward();    //    Start    the
animation when the screen is initialized
}

@override
void dispose() {
  _controller.dispose();  //  Clean  up  the
animation controller
  super.dispose();
}

@override
```

```
Widget build(BuildContext context) {
  return Scaffold(
    appBar:    AppBar(title:    Text('Weather
App')),
      body: Center(
        child: FadeTransition(
          opacity: _opacityAnimation,
          child: Column(
            mainAxisAlignment:
MainAxisAlignment.center,
            children: [
              Icon(Icons.wb_sunny, size: 100),
              SizedBox(height: 20),
              Text('Temperature: 25°C', style:
TextStyle(fontSize: 24)),
              SizedBox(height: 10),
              Text('Sunny',               style:
TextStyle(fontSize: 18)),
            ],
          ),
        ),
      ),
    );
  }
}
```

Step 2: Adding Animation for Weather Icon

We can animate the weather icon using a `RotationTransition` or a `ScaleTransition` to create a smooth visual effect when the weather data changes.

Summary

In this chapter, we covered:

- **Types of animations**: Implicit (e.g., `AnimatedContainer`, `AnimatedOpacity`) vs. Explicit (e.g., `AnimationController`, `Tween`).
- **Flutter's animation widgets**: We learned how to use `AnimatedContainer`, `AnimatedOpacity`, and `TweenAnimationBuilder` for simple animations.
- **Custom animations**: We explored how to create custom animations using `AnimationController`, `Tween`, and `AnimatedBuilder`.
- **Example**: We created a **weather app** that includes fade-in and smooth transitions for displaying weather data and icons.

With these tools, you can make your Flutter apps more dynamic and engaging by adding animations that improve the user experience.

CHAPTER 11

HANDLING USER INPUT –
FORMS AND VALIDATION

In this chapter, we will explore how to handle user input in Flutter, focusing on using **TextField** widgets and **Form** widgets to capture and validate data. User input is crucial for many apps, whether it's for signing up, logging in, submitting feedback, or filling out a survey. Properly validating and managing user input is key to ensuring data integrity and improving the user experience. By the end of this chapter, you will understand how to use forms and validation in Flutter and how to implement custom validation logic.

Working with TextFields and Form Widgets

TextField Widget

The `TextField` widget is used to capture text input from the user. It is highly customizable and can be styled to fit the needs of your app.

Here's a simple example of using a `TextField` to capture user input:

```dart
TextField(
  decoration: InputDecoration(
    labelText: 'Username',
    border: OutlineInputBorder(),
  ),
  onChanged: (text) {
    print('User entered: $text');
  },
)
```

In this example:

- The `decoration` property is used to style the `TextField`, adding a label and a border.
- The `onChanged` callback is triggered whenever the text in the field changes, allowing you to capture and react to user input.

Form Widget

The `Form` widget is a container for grouping multiple input fields, such as `TextFields`, and it provides functionality for **validating** and **saving** the data entered by the user.

You typically use the `Form` widget along with a **GlobalKey** to manage its state.

```dart
final _formKey = GlobalKey<FormState>();

Form(
  key: _formKey,
  child: Column(
    children: [
      TextFormField(
        decoration:   InputDecoration(labelText:
'Username'),
        validator: (value) {
          if (value == null || value.isEmpty) {
            return 'Please enter a username';
          }
          return null;
        },
      ),
      ElevatedButton(
        onPressed: () {
          if (_formKey.currentState?.validate()
?? false) {
            // Process data if validation passes
          }
        },
        child: Text('Submit'),
      ),
    ],
  ),
```

)

In this example:

- The `Form` widget is wrapped around the `TextFormField`.
- The `validator` property of the `TextFormField` checks whether the input is valid (e.g., not empty).
- The `_formKey` is used to access the state of the `Form` and trigger validation when the user submits the form.

Validating User Input

User input validation is crucial for ensuring that the data submitted by users is correct and consistent with the app's requirements. Flutter provides built-in validation for `TextFormField` widgets.

Basic Validation

The simplest form of validation involves checking if the input is not empty or null. You can define the validation logic using the `validator` property.

Example:

dart

```
TextFormField(
  decoration:           InputDecoration(labelText:
'Email'),
  validator: (value) {
    if (value == null || value.isEmpty) {
      return 'Please enter an email';
    }
    return null;
  },
)
```

Using Regular Expressions for Validation

You can also validate user input using regular expressions (regex). This is useful for more complex checks, such as validating an email address or phone number.

Example (Email Validation):

dart

```
TextFormField(
  decoration:           InputDecoration(labelText:
'Email'),
  validator: (value) {
    if (value == null || value.isEmpty) {
      return 'Please enter an email';
    }
    // Simple email regex pattern
```

```
final emailRegex = RegExp(r'^[a-zA-Z0-9._%+-
]+@[a-zA-Z0-9.-]+\.[a-zA-Z]{2,}$');
    if (!emailRegex.hasMatch(value)) {
      return 'Please enter a valid email
address';
    }
    return null;
  },
)
```

Here, the `validator` checks if the input matches a simple regular expression pattern for email validation.

Multiple Fields Validation

If you need to validate multiple fields (e.g., a password confirmation), you can use the `FormState`'s `validate()` method to validate all the fields at once.

Example (Password Confirmation):

dart

```
final            _passwordController            =
TextEditingController();
final          _confirmPasswordController          =
TextEditingController();

Form(
```

```
  key: _formKey,
  child: Column(
    children: [
      TextFormField(
        controller: _passwordController,
        decoration:    InputDecoration(labelText:
'Password'),
        obscureText: true,
        validator: (value) {
          if (value == null || value.isEmpty) {
            return 'Please enter a password';
          }
          return null;
        },
      ),
      TextFormField(
        controller: _confirmPasswordController,
        decoration:    InputDecoration(labelText:
'Confirm Password'),
        obscureText: true,
        validator: (value) {
          if (value == null || value.isEmpty) {
            return    'Please    confirm    your
password';
          }
          if (value != _passwordController.text)
{
            return 'Passwords do not match';
          }
```

```
        return null;
      },
    ),
    ElevatedButton(
      onPressed: () {
        if (_formKey.currentState?.validate()
?? false) {
          // Proceed with form submission if
validation passes
        }
      },
      child: Text('Submit'),
    ),
  ],
 ),
)
```

In this example:

- We use two `TextEditingController` objects to manage the password and confirm password fields.
- The confirm password field's validator checks if the input matches the password.

Custom Form Validation Logic

Sometimes, you may want to perform custom validation logic that is not directly tied to a specific field. You can create a custom

152

function to validate the entire form, or combine different field values for complex validation rules.

Example: **Username availability check** (using an API or a mock check):

dart

```
Future<String?> validateUsername(String value)
async {
  if (value.isEmpty) {
    return 'Please enter a username';
  }

  // Simulate a network call for username
availability
  await Future.delayed(Duration(seconds: 1));

  if (value == 'takenUsername') {
    return 'Username is already taken';
  }

  return null;
}

TextFormField(
  decoration:          InputDecoration(labelText:
'Username'),
  validator: (value) async {
```

153

```
      return await validateUsername(value ?? '');
    },
  )
)
```

In this example:

- The `validateUsername` function simulates an asynchronous check for username availability. If the username is taken, it returns an error message.

Example: Building a Registration Form with Input Validation

Let's build a simple **registration form** that validates user input for **name**, **email**, and **password** fields. We will use **TextFormField** widgets, validation logic, and a submit button that processes the input if all fields are valid.

dart

```
class RegistrationForm extends StatefulWidget {
  @override
  _RegistrationFormState    createState()    =>
_RegistrationFormState();
}

class      _RegistrationFormState      extends
State<RegistrationForm> {
  final _formKey = GlobalKey<FormState>();
```

```
  final          _nameController          =
TextEditingController();
  final          _emailController          =
TextEditingController();
  final          _passwordController          =
TextEditingController();


  @override
  Widget build(BuildContext context) {
    return Scaffold(
      appBar:                    AppBar(title:
Text('Registration')),
      body: Padding(
        padding: EdgeInsets.all(16.0),
        child: Form(
          key: _formKey,
          child: Column(
            children: [
              // Name Field
              TextFormField(
                controller: _nameController,
                decoration:
InputDecoration(labelText: 'Name'),
                validator: (value) {
                  if   (value   ==   null   ||
value.isEmpty) {
                    return 'Please enter your
name';
                  }
```

```
                return null;
              },
            ),
            SizedBox(height: 20),
            // Email Field
            TextFormField(
              controller: _emailController,
              decoration:
InputDecoration(labelText: 'Email'),
              validator: (value) {
                if (value == null ||
value.isEmpty) {
                  return 'Please enter your
email';
                }
                final emailRegex =
RegExp(r'^[a-zA-Z0-9._%+-]+@[a-zA-Z0-9.-]+\.[a-
zA-Z]{2,}$');
                if
(!emailRegex.hasMatch(value)) {
                  return 'Please enter a valid
email address';
                }
                return null;
              },
            ),
            SizedBox(height: 20),
            // Password Field
            TextFormField(
```

156

```
              controller: _passwordController,
              obscureText: true,
              decoration:
InputDecoration(labelText: 'Password'),
              validator: (value) {
                 if    (value    ==    null    ||
value.isEmpty) {
                     return    'Please    enter    a
password';
                 }
                 if (value.length < 6) {
                     return 'Password must be at
least 6 characters';
                 }
                 return null;
              },
           ),
           SizedBox(height: 40),
           // Submit Button
           ElevatedButton(
             onPressed: () {
                if
(_formKey.currentState?.validate() ?? false) {
                     //    Process    data    if
validation passes

ScaffoldMessenger.of(context).showSnackBar(
                     SnackBar(content:
Text('Processing Data')),
```

```
                );
              }
            },
            child: Text('Register'),
          ),
        ],
      ),
    ),
  ),
);
  }
}
```

Key Points:

- **Validation**: We validate each field using the `validator` property of `TextFormField`.
- **Submit Button**: When the user presses the submit button, we call `validate()` on the form. If all fields are valid, the form can be processed (e.g., saving data or calling an API).

158

Summary

In this chapter, we covered:

- **TextField** and **Form** widgets for handling user input in Flutter.
- **Validating user input** using built-in validators and regular expressions.
- **Custom form validation logic** for more complex validation requirements.
- A **real-world example** of building a registration form with input validation.

By mastering these techniques, you can ensure that your app handles user input efficiently and correctly, providing a smooth and reliable experience for your users.

CHAPTER 12

MANAGING APP LIFE CYCLE AND RESOURCES

In this chapter, we will explore how to manage your Flutter app's lifecycle, handle background tasks, and manage app resources such as images, icons, and fonts. Understanding how to manage the app's lifecycle and resources is critical for building efficient, responsive, and resource-friendly apps. We will also walk through an example of building a **music player app** that handles background audio, which requires managing the app's lifecycle and resources.

Understanding the App Lifecycle in Flutter

The app lifecycle refers to the stages in the life of your app, from when it is launched to when it is closed. Managing the app lifecycle is crucial to ensure your app performs well and behaves as expected in different situations, such as when the app goes to the background or is reopened after being paused.

Flutter provides several ways to manage and listen for lifecycle events using the `WidgetsBindingObserver` mixin.

App Lifecycle States

Flutter apps go through several lifecycle states, which are defined by the **AppLifecycleState** enum. The main states are:

1. **Resumed**: The app is in the foreground, actively running.
2. **Inactive**: The app is in the foreground but is not receiving user input (e.g., when a phone call is received).
3. **Paused**: The app is not visible (e.g., the app goes to the background).
4. **Detached**: The app is still in memory but not attached to the UI (this state is rarely used).

You can listen to these states by adding the WidgetsBindingObserver to your State class:

dart

```
class MyAppState extends State<MyApp> with
WidgetsBindingObserver {
  @override
  void initState() {
    super.initState();
    WidgetsBinding.instance?.addObserver(this);
  }

  @override
  void dispose() {
```

```dart
WidgetsBinding.instance?.removeObserver(this);
    super.dispose();
  }


  @override
  void
didChangeAppLifecycleState(AppLifecycleState
state) {
    super.didChangeAppLifecycleState(state);
    if (state == AppLifecycleState.paused) {
      print("App paused");
      // Handle app pause (e.g., stop background
music)
    } else if (state ==
AppLifecycleState.resumed) {
      print("App resumed");
      // Handle app resume (e.g., restart
background music)
    }
  }


  @override
  Widget build(BuildContext context) {
    return MaterialApp(
      home: Scaffold(
        appBar: AppBar(title: Text('App
Lifecycle Example')),
```

```
        body:    Center(child:    Text('App    is
running')),
        ),
    );
  }
}
```

In this example:

- We listen for lifecycle state changes and handle the **pause** and **resume** events.
- We use `WidgetsBinding.instance?.addObserver(this)` to start listening for lifecycle changes and `dispose()` to stop listening when the widget is disposed.

Handling App Pauses, Resume, and Background Tasks

When the app goes into the background or is paused, you may want to perform certain tasks, such as saving data, stopping audio, or releasing resources. Similarly, when the app is resumed, you may want to refresh data or restart tasks.

Handling App Pause

When the app is paused, it might be due to the user navigating away from the app, or the app being put into the background (e.g., when the user switches to another app). Use the lifecycle state `AppLifecycleState.paused` to manage these scenarios.

Example: Stopping background audio when the app is paused.

dart

```
@override
void
didChangeAppLifecycleState(AppLifecycleState
state) {
  if (state == AppLifecycleState.paused) {
    // Pause the audio player when the app is
paused
    _audioPlayer.pause();
  }
}
```

Handling App Resume

When the app is resumed, you may want to restart background tasks, refresh data, or continue a previously interrupted operation.

Example: Resuming audio when the app is resumed.

dart

```
@override
```

```
void
didChangeAppLifecycleState(AppLifecycleState
state) {
  if (state == AppLifecycleState.resumed) {
    // Resume audio playback when the app is
resumed
    _audioPlayer.play();
  }
}
```

Handling Background Tasks

Handling background tasks (such as playing audio, fetching data, or handling notifications) is important for apps that need to continue working even when they are not actively in the foreground.

Flutter provides the `flutter_background_service` package for running background tasks. This package allows you to perform background operations like fetching data or playing audio while the app is not active.

Example: Playing audio in the background using the `flutter_background_service` plugin.

```yaml
yaml

dependencies:
  flutter_background_service: ^0.1.2
  audio_service: ^0.18.1
```

Managing Resources (Images, Icons, Fonts)

Flutter provides various ways to manage app resources such as images, icons, and fonts. Efficient resource management is essential for optimizing app performance and reducing the app's size.

Managing Images

To add images to your app, you must place them in the `assets` folder and reference them in the `pubspec.yaml` file.

1. **Adding Images to Assets:**

yaml

```
flutter:
  assets:
    - assets/images/
```

2. **Using Images in Widgets:**

You can load and display images in Flutter using the `Image.asset` or `Image.network` widgets.

Example:

dart

```
Image.asset('assets/images/logo.png')
```

Managing Icons

Flutter comes with a large set of predefined icons in the `Icons` class, but you can also use custom icons by adding them to your `assets` folder and referencing them in your code.

Example: Using a predefined icon:

```
dart
```

```
Icon(Icons.music_note, size: 50)
```

To use custom icons, you would add the icon files to your `assets` folder and load them using `ImageIcon`.

Example:

```
dart
```

```
ImageIcon(AssetImage('assets/icons/music_icon.png'))
```

Managing Fonts

You can add custom fonts to your Flutter app by placing them in the `assets/fonts` folder and referencing them in the `pubspec.yaml` file.

1. **Adding Fonts:**

yaml

```
flutter:
  fonts:
    - family: Roboto
      fonts:
        - asset: assets/fonts/Roboto-Regular.ttf
        - asset: assets/fonts/Roboto-Bold.ttf
          weight: 700
```

2. **Using Custom Fonts in Widgets:**

You can apply the custom font to your Text widgets:

dart

```
Text(
  'Custom Font Example',
  style: TextStyle(fontFamily: 'Roboto'),
)
```

Example: Building a Music Player App that Handles Background Audio

Let's create a simple **music player app** that handles background audio. This app will play music, pause the music when the app is minimized, and resume playback when the app is opened again.

Step 1: Add Dependencies

First, add the required dependencies for audio playback and background services in your `pubspec.yaml` file:

yaml

```
dependencies:
  flutter:
    sdk: flutter
  audioplayers: ^0.20.1
  flutter_background_service: ^0.1.2
```

Step 2: Initialize Audio Player

dart

```
import 'package:audioplayers/audioplayers.dart';
import 'package:flutter/material.dart';

class MusicPlayerApp extends StatefulWidget {
  @override
  _MusicPlayerAppState      createState()       =>
_MusicPlayerAppState();
}

class      _MusicPlayerAppState      extends
State<MusicPlayerApp>                   with
WidgetsBindingObserver {
  final     AudioPlayer     _audioPlayer     =
AudioPlayer();
```

```
@override
void initState() {
  super.initState();
  WidgetsBinding.instance?.addObserver(this);
}

@override
void dispose() {
  _audioPlayer.dispose();

WidgetsBinding.instance?.removeObserver(this);
  super.dispose();
}

@override
void
didChangeAppLifecycleState(AppLifecycleState
state) {
    if (state == AppLifecycleState.paused) {
     _audioPlayer.pause(); // Pause the audio
when the app goes to the background
    } else if (state ==
AppLifecycleState.resumed) {
     _audioPlayer.resume(); // Resume the audio
when the app comes back to the foreground
    }
  }
```

```
@override
Widget build(BuildContext context) {
  return MaterialApp(
    home: Scaffold(
      appBar:    AppBar(title:    Text('Music
Player')),
        body: Center(
          child: Column(
            mainAxisAlignment:
MainAxisAlignment.center,
              children: [
                ElevatedButton(
                  onPressed: () {

_audioPlayer.play('https://www.soundhelix.com/e
xamples/mp3/SoundHelix-Song-1.mp3');
                  },
                  child: Text('Play Music'),
                ),
                ElevatedButton(
                  onPressed: () {
                    _audioPlayer.pause();
                  },
                  child: Text('Pause Music'),
                ),
              ],
          ),
        ),
      ),
```

```
    );
  }
}
```

In this example:

- We use the `audioplayers` package to handle music playback.
- The app pauses the audio when the app goes to the background and resumes it when the app comes back to the foreground.

Summary

In this chapter, we covered:

- **Managing the app lifecycle** using `WidgetsBindingObserver` to handle app pauses, resumes, and background tasks.
- **Managing resources** like images, icons, and fonts to optimize performance and keep the app's assets organized.
- **Building a music player app** that handles background audio by pausing and resuming playback based on the app's lifecycle state.

By mastering these concepts, you can build efficient apps that respond to lifecycle changes, optimize resource usage, and provide a better user experience.

CHAPTER 13

IMPLEMENTING PUSH NOTIFICATIONS

Push notifications are a crucial feature for engaging users in real-time, keeping them informed about new events, messages, or updates, even when they are not actively using the app. In this chapter, we will dive into **push notifications**, set up **Firebase Cloud Messaging (FCM)** to send and receive notifications, and build a real-world example of adding push notifications to a **messaging app**.

What Are Push Notifications?

Push notifications are messages sent from a server to a mobile device. These messages appear even if the app is not running, allowing apps to deliver updates or alerts to users. Push notifications can be used for various purposes:

- **Alerting users about new messages**, emails, or events.
- **Sending reminders** for scheduled tasks or updates.
- **Promoting new content**, offers, or updates within the app.

- **Re-engaging inactive users** by sending personalized content or notifications.

Push notifications are a powerful tool to increase user engagement and retention. They work by establishing a persistent connection between the app and a server, and the server sends notifications to the device when certain events occur.

Setting Up Firebase Cloud Messaging (FCM)

To implement push notifications in Flutter, we use **Firebase Cloud Messaging (FCM)**. FCM allows you to send notifications to your users across platforms like Android and iOS.

Step 1: Set Up Firebase for Your Flutter Project

1. **Go to Firebase Console**: Navigate to Firebase Console and create a new project.
2. **Add Your Flutter App to Firebase**:
   - Select your project and click on "Add app".
   - Choose the platform (Android or iOS) and follow the instructions to configure Firebase for your app.
   - For Android, you'll need to download the google-services.json file and place it in the android/app/ directory of your Flutter project.

175

o For iOS, you'll need to configure the app with Firebase using `GoogleService-Info.plist` and enable push notifications in the Xcode project settings.

Step 2: Add Dependencies

To integrate Firebase Cloud Messaging with Flutter, add the following dependencies to your `pubspec.yaml` file:

yaml

```yaml
dependencies:
  flutter:
    sdk: flutter
  firebase_core: ^1.10.0
  firebase_messaging: ^10.0.0
```

Then, run `flutter pub get` to install the dependencies.

Step 3: Initialize Firebase in Your App

You need to initialize Firebase when the app starts. In your `main.dart` file, ensure Firebase is initialized before the app runs:

dart

```dart
import
'package:firebase_core/firebase_core.dart';
```

```dart
import 'package:flutter/material.dart';

void main() async {
  WidgetsFlutterBinding.ensureInitialized();
  await Firebase.initializeApp();  // Initialize
Firebase
  runApp(MyApp());
}

class MyApp extends StatelessWidget {
  @override
  Widget build(BuildContext context) {
    return MaterialApp(
      title: 'Flutter Push Notifications',
      home: HomeScreen(),
    );
  }
}
```

Step 4: Configure Firebase Messaging

Now that Firebase is initialized, let's set up Firebase Cloud Messaging in your app.

1. **Configure Firebase Messaging for Android**:
   o Open `android/app/build.gradle` and ensure the following line is included:

   ```
   gradle
   ```

```
apply                    plugin:
'com.google.gms.google-services'
```

o In the `android/build.gradle` file, make sure the Google services classpath is added:

```
gradle

classpath    'com.google.gms:google-
services:4.3.10'
```

2. **Configure Firebase Messaging for iOS**:

o In Xcode, enable **Push Notifications** in your app's capabilities.

o Modify the `Info.plist` file to include necessary permissions for push notifications.

Sending and Receiving Notifications

Once you have set up Firebase Cloud Messaging, you can start sending and receiving push notifications.

Step 1: Request Permission to Receive Notifications

For iOS, you need to request permission to show notifications. On Android, this is handled automatically.

Add the following code to request notification permissions on iOS:

dart

```dart
import
'package:firebase_messaging/firebase_messaging.
dart';

Future<void> requestPermission() async {
  FirebaseMessaging        messaging        =
FirebaseMessaging.instance;

  NotificationSettings    settings    =    await
messaging.requestPermission(
    alert: true,
    badge: true,
    sound: true,
  );

  if      (settings.authorizationStatus    ==
AuthorizationStatus.authorized) {
    print('User    granted    permission    for
notifications');
  } else {
    print('User declined or has not accepted
notification permission');
  }
}
```

You can call `requestPermission()` in your app's initialization process (e.g., in `initState()`).

Step 2: Handle Foreground Notifications

You can handle notifications while the app is in the foreground using the `FirebaseMessaging.onMessage` stream.

Example:

dart

```
FirebaseMessaging.onMessage.listen((RemoteMessa
ge message) {
   print('Message                    received:
${message.notification?.title}');
   // Show a local notification, update UI, or
trigger other actions
});
```

Step 3: Handle Background and Terminated State Notifications

When the app is in the background or terminated, the system will automatically display notifications. You can handle these notifications by setting up background message handlers.

For background messages:

dart

```
Future<void>      backgroundHandler(RemoteMessage
message) async {
  print('Handling    a    background    message:
${message.notification?.title}');
}


FirebaseMessaging.onBackgroundMessage(backgroun
dHandler);
```

Step 4: Sending Notifications from Firebase Console

To send a test push notification from Firebase:

1. Go to Firebase Console > Cloud Messaging.
2. Click "Send Your First Message".
3. Add the message title, body, and any custom data you want to send.
4. Select the target app and send the notification.

Real-World Example: Adding Push Notifications to a Messaging App

Let's integrate push notifications into a **messaging app**. The app will send a notification when a new message is received, even when the app is not in the foreground.

Step 1: Set Up the Messaging App UI

Create a basic messaging UI with a list of messages:

dart

```dart
class MessageScreen extends StatefulWidget {
  @override
  _MessageScreenState createState() =>
_MessageScreenState();
}


class _MessageScreenState extends
State<MessageScreen> {
  final FirebaseMessaging _firebaseMessaging =
FirebaseMessaging.instance;
  final List<String> _messages = [];


  @override
  void initState() {
    super.initState();

_firebaseMessaging.subscribeToTopic("chat");
    _listenForMessages();
  }


  // Listen for new messages while the app is in
the foreground
  void _listenForMessages() {
```

```
FirebaseMessaging.onMessage.listen((RemoteMessa
ge message) {
      setState(() {

_messages.add(message.notification?.title    ??
'New Message');
      });
    });
  }

  @override
  Widget build(BuildContext context) {
    return Scaffold(
      appBar: AppBar(title: Text('Messages')),
      body: ListView.builder(
        itemCount: _messages.length,
        itemBuilder: (context, index) {
          return ListTile(
            title: Text(_messages[index]),
          );
        },
      ),
    );
  }
}
```

In this example:

- We subscribe to a topic (e.g., `"chat"`) to receive notifications for new messages.
- When a notification is received while the app is in the foreground, we update the message list.

Step 2: Send Notifications on New Message

When a user sends a new message, you can trigger a push notification using Firebase Cloud Messaging. If your app sends messages via Firebase Cloud Functions or a backend, you can use Firebase Cloud Messaging's HTTP API to send a message.

Example using the Firebase Cloud Functions to send a push notification:

```javascript
const admin = require('firebase-admin');
admin.initializeApp();

exports.sendMessageNotification =
functions.firestore
    .document('messages/{messageId}')
    .onCreate((snapshot, context) => {
        const message = snapshot.data();
        const payload = {
            notification: {
                title: 'New Message',
                body: message.text,
```

```
        },
    };

    // Send notification to all users
subscribed to "chat" topic
    return
admin.messaging().sendToTopic('chat', payload);
  });
```

In this example, we listen for new messages stored in Firestore and trigger a push notification to the "chat" topic.

Summary

In this chapter, we covered:

- **Push notifications** and their use in mobile apps to engage users in real-time.
- **Setting up Firebase Cloud Messaging (FCM),** including setting up Firebase for Flutter, configuring permissions, and handling notifications.
- **Sending and receiving notifications**: We demonstrated how to receive notifications while the app is in the foreground and background.

- A **real-world example**: We added push notifications to a messaging app, allowing users to be notified of new messages even when the app is not in the foreground.

By mastering push notifications, you can significantly improve user engagement, making your app more interactive and timely.

CHAPTER 14

INTEGRATING WITH FIREBASE – FIREBASE ESSENTIALS

Firebase is a powerful and popular platform for building mobile and web applications. It provides a variety of backend services, including databases, authentication, analytics, and more, all with easy integration into your app. In this chapter, we'll walk through how to integrate **Firebase** into a Flutter app, covering essential Firebase features like **user authentication** and **Firestore**, a real-time NoSQL database.

What is Firebase and Why Use It in Mobile Apps?

Firebase is a backend-as-a-service (BaaS) platform developed by Google. It provides cloud-based services to help developers build apps quickly and easily. Firebase can be used to manage your app's data, user authentication, push notifications, and much more.

Why use Firebase in mobile apps?

- **Easy Integration**: Firebase provides SDKs for various platforms, including Flutter, making it easy to integrate backend services with your mobile app.

- **Real-time Database**: Firebase's Firestore database offers real-time syncing, making it ideal for apps that require real-time updates, like chat apps, social media, or collaborative apps.
- **Authentication**: Firebase Authentication supports multiple sign-in methods like email/password, Google, Facebook, and more, simplifying user authentication.
- **Scalability**: Firebase is built on Google's cloud infrastructure, offering automatic scaling to handle millions of users without the need for manual configuration.
- **Cross-Platform Support**: Firebase supports Android, iOS, and web, allowing you to use the same backend across platforms.

Setting Up Firebase for Flutter

To get started with Firebase in Flutter, you'll need to set up a Firebase project and integrate Firebase SDKs into your Flutter app.

Step 1: Create a Firebase Project

1. Go to Firebase Console and create a new Firebase project.

2. Once your project is created, select the platform (Android/iOS) and follow the instructions to add your app to Firebase.

3. Download the configuration files:

   o **For Android**, download google-services.json and place it in the android/app/ directory of your Flutter project.

   o **For iOS**, download GoogleService-Info.plist and add it to the ios/Runner/ directory.

Step 2: Add Firebase Dependencies

Next, add the necessary Firebase packages to your pubspec.yaml file. For Firebase Authentication and Firestore, add the following dependencies:

yaml

```
dependencies:
  flutter:
    sdk: flutter
  firebase_core: ^1.10.0
  firebase_auth: ^3.1.6
  cloud_firestore: ^3.1.5
```

Run flutter pub get to install the dependencies.

Step 3: Initialize Firebase

You need to initialize Firebase when the app starts. Add the following code in the `main.dart` file to initialize Firebase:

```dart
import
'package:firebase_core/firebase_core.dart';
import 'package:flutter/material.dart';

void main() async {
  WidgetsFlutterBinding.ensureInitialized();
  await Firebase.initializeApp();  // Initialize
Firebase
  runApp(MyApp());
}

class MyApp extends StatelessWidget {
  @override
  Widget build(BuildContext context) {
    return MaterialApp(
      title: 'Firebase Flutter App',
      home: HomeScreen(),
    );
  }
}
```

In the above code:

- `Firebase.initializeApp()` is called in the `main()` function to initialize Firebase before the app starts.

Using Firebase Auth for User Authentication

Firebase Authentication provides an easy way to authenticate users with various methods, including email/password, Google, Facebook, and more.

Step 1: Setting Up Firebase Auth

To authenticate users with Firebase, you can use the `firebase_auth` package.

```dart
import
'package:firebase_auth/firebase_auth.dart';

final        FirebaseAuth        _auth        =
FirebaseAuth.instance;

// Sign up with email and password
Future<User?>      signUpWithEmailPassword(String
email, String password) async {
  try {
    final UserCredential userCredential = await
_auth.createUserWithEmailAndPassword(
```

191

```
      email: email,
      password: password,
    );
    return userCredential.user;
  } catch (e) {
    print("Error signing up: $e");
    return null;
  }
}


// Sign in with email and password
Future<User?>     signInWithEmailPassword(String
email, String password) async {
  try {
    final UserCredential userCredential = await
_auth.signInWithEmailAndPassword(
      email: email,
      password: password,
    );
    return userCredential.user;
  } catch (e) {
    print("Error signing in: $e");
    return null;
  }
}
```

Step 2: Implementing the Sign-Up and Login UI

You can now implement the sign-up and login UI to capture user credentials and authenticate them.

Example for a simple sign-up form:

```dart
dart

class SignUpScreen extends StatefulWidget {
  @override
  _SignUpScreenState      createState()      =>
_SignUpScreenState();
}

class      _SignUpScreenState      extends
State<SignUpScreen> {
  final TextEditingController _emailController =
TextEditingController();
  final             TextEditingController
_passwordController = TextEditingController();

  Future<void> _signUp() async {
    final email = _emailController.text;
    final password = _passwordController.text;

    User?      user      =      await
signUpWithEmailPassword(email, password);
    if (user != null) {
      print("User signed up: ${user.email}");
      // Navigate to home screen
    } else {
      print("Sign-up failed");
    }
  }
```

```
@override
Widget build(BuildContext context) {
  return Scaffold(
    appBar: AppBar(title: Text("Sign Up")),
    body: Padding(
      padding: EdgeInsets.all(16.0),
      child: Column(
        children: [
          TextField(
            controller: _emailController,
            decoration:
InputDecoration(labelText: "Email"),
          ),
          TextField(
            controller: _passwordController,
            obscureText: true,
            decoration:
InputDecoration(labelText: "Password"),
          ),
          ElevatedButton(
            onPressed: _signUp,
            child: Text("Sign Up"),
          ),
        ],
      ),
    ),
  );
}
```

}

In this example:

- The `signUpWithEmailPassword` function handles creating a user with the given email and password.
- We capture user input using `TextEditingControllers` and pass them to the `signUpWithEmailPassword` method.

Step 3: Handling User Sign-In

Similarly, you can implement the sign-in functionality using `signInWithEmailPassword` in the login screen.

Using Firebase Firestore for Real-Time Database

Firebase Firestore is a NoSQL document database that allows you to store and sync data in real-time across all devices. It's perfect for apps that need real-time collaboration or updates, like messaging apps, social media apps, or collaborative document editing.

Step 1: Add Firestore Dependencies

Make sure you have the `cloud_firestore` dependency in your `pubspec.yaml` file (which you already added in Step 2).

```dart
import
'package:cloud_firestore/cloud_firestore.dart';

final   FirebaseFirestore   _firestore   =
FirebaseFirestore.instance;

// Add a new document
Future<void> addMessage(String message) async {
  await _firestore.collection('messages').add({
    'message': message,
    'createdAt': FieldValue.serverTimestamp(),
  });
}

// Get all documents in the 'messages' collection
Stream<List<String>> getMessages() {
  return _firestore
      .collection('messages')
      .orderBy('createdAt', descending: true)
      .snapshots()
      .map((snapshot) {
    return snapshot.docs.map((doc)   =>
doc['message'] as String).toList();
  });
}
```

Step 2: Adding and Fetching Messages

You can add messages to Firestore and listen for real-time updates using `StreamBuilder`. Here's an example of how to build a messaging interface that displays messages from Firestore:

dart

```
class ChatScreen extends StatelessWidget {
  final TextEditingController _messageController
= TextEditingController();

  @override
  Widget build(BuildContext context) {
    return Scaffold(
      appBar: AppBar(title: Text('Chat')),
      body: Column(
        children: [
          Expanded(
            child: StreamBuilder<List<String>>(
              stream: getMessages(),
              builder: (context, snapshot) {
                if (snapshot.connectionState ==
ConnectionState.waiting) {
                  return          Center(child:
CircularProgressIndicator());
                }

                if (snapshot.hasError) {
```

```
            return           Center(child:
Text('Error: ${snapshot.error}'));
            }

            final messages = snapshot.data
?? [];

            return ListView.builder(
              itemCount: messages.length,
              itemBuilder: (context, index)
{
                return ListTile(
                  title:
Text(messages[index]),
                );
              },
            );
          },
        ),
      ),
      Padding(
        padding: const EdgeInsets.all(8.0),
        child: Row(
          children: [
            Expanded(
              child: TextField(
                controller:
_messageController,
```

```
                    decoration:
InputDecoration(labelText: 'Message'),
                      ),
                    ),
                 IconButton(
                    icon: Icon(Icons.send),
                    onPressed: () async {
                      if
(_messageController.text.isNotEmpty) {
                         await
addMessage(_messageController.text);

_messageController.clear();
                      }
                    },
                  ),
               ],
             ),
           ),
         ],
       ),
     );
   }
}
```

In this example:

- We use **StreamBuilder** to listen for real-time updates from Firestore.

- New messages are added to Firestore and displayed in real-time without requiring manual refresh.

Example: Building a User Authentication System with Firebase

In the previous steps, we learned how to integrate Firebase Auth for signing up and logging in users. Combining this with Firestore allows you to create a complete user authentication system with a user database.

1. **Create a collection to store user profiles**:
   - When a user signs up, create a document in the Firestore database for their profile, storing basic information like name, email, and profile picture.
2. **Secure data access**:
   - Use Firebase rules to secure user data. For example, only allow users to read/write their own data by using `auth.uid` in Firestore rules.

Summary

In this chapter, we covered the essentials of integrating Firebase into your Flutter app, including:

- **Setting up Firebase for Flutter** and initializing Firebase in your app.
- **Firebase Auth** for user authentication with methods like sign-up and sign-in.
- **Firestore** for real-time data storage, including adding, retrieving, and displaying messages.
- A **real-world example** of building a user authentication system with Firebase and Firestore.

With Firebase, you can easily add powerful backend services like authentication, real-time databases, and cloud storage, helping you focus on building the core features of your app.

CHAPTER 15

BUILDING AND DEPLOYING APPS FOR ANDROID AND IOS

In this chapter, we will focus on the steps involved in building and deploying your Flutter app for **Android** and **iOS** platforms. You will learn how to configure your app for both platforms, sign and release your app to the **Google Play Store** and **Apple App Store**, and manage app versions and updates. We will also walk through a **real-world example** to prepare an app for deployment.

Building Android and iOS Apps with Flutter

Flutter allows you to build cross-platform mobile apps with a single codebase. However, each platform (Android and iOS) has its own requirements for building and deploying apps. Let's go over the general process for building an app for each platform.

1. Building the Android App

To build your Flutter app for Android, follow these steps:

1. **Ensure Android SDK is installed**:

o Make sure you have **Android Studio** installed and the Android SDK set up correctly. You can verify the installation by running `flutter doctor` in the terminal.

2. **Configure the app for Android**:

   o The `android` folder in your Flutter project contains all the configuration files for the Android app. You can configure things like the app's version, application ID, and permissions in the `android/app/build.gradle` file.

3. **Build the APK or AAB**:

   o **APK (Android Package)** is the file format for Android apps. You can generate it by running:

   ```bash
   ```

   ```
   flutter build apk --release
   ```

   o **AAB (Android App Bundle)** is the recommended file format for publishing apps on the Google Play Store. You can generate it by running:

   ```bash
   ```

   ```
   flutter build appbundle --release
   ```

4. **Verify the app**:

o After building the APK or AAB, you can install it on your Android device for testing.

```bash
```

```
flutter install
```

2. Building the iOS App

To build your Flutter app for iOS, follow these steps:

1. **Ensure Xcode is installed**:
    o Make sure you have **Xcode** installed on your macOS system, as it is required to build and deploy iOS apps. You can verify the installation by running `flutter doctor`.

2. **Configure the app for iOS**:
    o The `ios` folder in your Flutter project contains all the configuration files for the iOS app. You can configure things like the app's bundle identifier, version, and deployment target in the `ios/Runner.xcodeproj` file.

3. **Build the iOS app**:
    o To build the app for iOS, use the following command:

```bash
```

```
flutter build ios --release
```

204

- o This command builds a release version of the app for iOS. You can run it on an iOS device or simulator to test it.

4. **Verify the app**:

- o After building the app, you can open the `.xcworkspace` file in Xcode and use the Xcode simulator or an actual iOS device to test the app.

Signing and Releasing Your App to the Google Play Store and Apple App Store

Once you've built and tested your app, it's time to sign and release it to the app stores. This process ensures that your app is properly authenticated and can be installed by users.

1. Signing and Releasing the Android App

To release your app on the **Google Play Store**, you need to sign your APK or AAB with a secure key.

1. **Generate a Keystore for Signing**:

- o Open a terminal and generate a keystore using the following command:

```bash
bash
```

```
keytool -genkey -v -keystore <your-
keystore-name>.keystore -keyalg RSA
-keysize 2048 -validity 10000 -alias
<your-key-alias>
```

o   This will create a keystore file that you can use to sign your APK or AAB.

2. **Configure Gradle to Use the Keystore**:

o   Open the `android/key.properties` file and add the following:

```
properties
```

```
storePassword=<your-keystore-
password>
keyPassword=<your-key-password>
keyAlias=<your-key-alias>
storeFile=<path-to-your-keystore>
```

o   Then,   update   the `android/app/build.gradle` file to reference the keystore:

```
gradle
```

```
signingConfigs {
  release {
    storeFile   file('<path-to-your-
keystore>')
```

206

```
    storePassword    '<your-keystore-
password>'
    keyAlias '<your-key-alias>'
    keyPassword              '<your-key-
password>'
  }
}

buildTypes {
  release {
    signingConfig
signingConfigs.release
  }
}
```

3. **Build the Signed APK or AAB**:

   o   After configuring the signing details, run the following command to build the signed APK or AAB:

   ```
   bash

   flutter build appbundle --release
   ```

   o   This will generate a signed `.aab` file that you can upload to the Google Play Console.

4. **Upload to Google Play Store**:

   o   Go to the Google Play Console and sign in with your developer account.

o Create a new app or select an existing one.

o Upload the `.aab` file, fill out the necessary metadata (description, screenshots, etc.), and submit your app for review.

2. Signing and Releasing the iOS App

To release your app on the **Apple App Store**, you need to sign your app using your Apple Developer account and a provisioning profile.

1. **Create an Apple Developer Account**:
   o You need an Apple Developer account to sign and release your app on the App Store. You can enroll in the Apple Developer Program for a yearly fee.

2. **Create a Distribution Certificate**:
   o Open **Xcode** and go to **Preferences** > **Accounts**.
   o Add your Apple ID and create a **distribution certificate** for your app.

3. **Create a Provisioning Profile**:
   o In your Apple Developer account, create a **provisioning profile** for distribution. This profile ensures that the app is authorized to run on user devices.

4. **Configure Xcode for Distribution**:

o Open the `ios/Runner.xcworkspace` file in Xcode.

o In the Xcode project settings, select your **Team** and configure the **Signing & Capabilities** tab to use your distribution certificate and provisioning profile.

5. **Build and Archive the App**:

o In Xcode, select **Generic iOS Device** as the target device and click **Product** > **Archive** to build the app.

o Once the app is archived, use **Xcode Organizer** to upload the app to the App Store.

6. **Upload to Apple App Store**:

o Log in to the Apple App Store Connect portal with your developer account.

o Select **My Apps** > + to create a new app or update an existing app.

o Upload the `.ipa` file generated in Xcode, fill out the necessary app details (app name, description, screenshots, etc.), and submit your app for review.

Managing App Versions and Updates

Once your app is live on the app stores, you will need to manage versions and updates.

1. Versioning Your App

Both Google Play Store and Apple App Store require that you specify a version number for your app. The version number is a string that is used to track app updates.

- **Android**: The version number is specified in the `android/app/build.gradle` file:

```gradle
versionCode: 1
versionName: "1.0.0"
```

  - **versionCode**: An integer that represents the version of your app. It must be incremented with each release.
  - **versionName**: A string representing the version name, visible to users (e.g., "1.0.0").
- **iOS**: The version number is specified in the `ios/Runner.xcodeproj` file:
  - **CFBundleShortVersionString**: Represents the version number (e.g., "1.0.0").
  - **CFBundleVersion**: Represents the build number (e.g., "1").

2. Updating Your App

When you release updates, increment the version number for both Android and iOS. The process for releasing updates is similar to releasing the initial app.

1. **Android**:
   - Update the `versionCode` and `versionName` in the `build.gradle` file.
   - Build and upload a new `.aab` file to the Google Play Console.
2. **iOS**:
   - Increment the `CFBundleShortVersionString` and `CFBundleVersion` in Xcode.
   - Archive and upload the new version to the App Store using Xcode.

Real-World Example: Preparing an App for Deployment

Let's assume we are preparing a **simple todo list app** for deployment.

1. **Build the app for Android and iOS**:
   - Follow the steps to build the release version for both platforms using `flutter build apk --`

release (Android) and flutter build ios --release (iOS).

2. **Sign the app for Android and iOS**:

   o Generate the keystore and configure the build.gradle for Android.

   o Set up the distribution certificate and provisioning profile for iOS.

3. **Upload to the App Stores**:

   o Upload the .aab to the **Google Play Store** and .ipa to the **Apple App Store**.

4. **Monitor the App**:

   o Once your app is live, monitor the reviews, crashes, and analytics from the Google Play Console and Apple App Store Connect.

Summary

In this chapter, we covered:

- **Building Android and iOS apps with Flutter**, including the necessary steps to build for both platforms.

- **Signing and releasing** your app to the **Google Play Store** and **Apple App Store**, including generating keystores and provisioning profiles.

- **Managing app versions** and **updates**, ensuring that each release is correctly versioned and uploaded.
- A **real-world example** of preparing an app for deployment, including the steps needed to release a simple app to both app stores.

With these steps, you can now confidently build, sign, and release your Flutter app to both Android and iOS platforms, ensuring it is ready for users worldwide.

CHAPTER 16

WORKING WITH GEOLOCATION AND MAPS

In this chapter, we will explore how to integrate **geolocation services** and **maps** into your Flutter app. Geolocation functionality is essential for location-based services such as ride-sharing apps, maps, and geo-targeted notifications. We'll cover using **location services** to fetch the user's current location and **Google Maps** to display maps and pins. Finally, we will walk through a **real-world example** of building a **location-based app** with a map interface.

Using Location Services in Flutter

To access the user's location in Flutter, we can use the **geolocator** package, which allows us to get the device's current location and monitor location changes.

Step 1: Add Dependencies

To get started, you need to add the **geolocator** and **google_maps_flutter** packages to your pubspec.yaml file:

```
yaml

dependencies:
  flutter:
    sdk: flutter
  geolocator: ^8.0.0
  google_maps_flutter: ^2.1.1
```

After updating the dependencies, run `flutter pub get` to install them.

Step 2: Request Permissions

Before accessing location services, you need to request permissions to access the device's location.

- **For Android**: In the `android/app/src/main/AndroidManifest.xml` file, add the following permissions:

```xml
xml

<uses-permission
android:name="android.permission.ACCESS_F
INE_LOCATION" />
<uses-permission
android:name="android.permission.ACCESS_C
OARSE_LOCATION" />
```

- **For iOS**: In the `ios/Runner/Info.plist` file, add:

215

```xml
<key>NSLocationWhenInUseUsageDescription<
/key>
<string>We    need    your    location    to    show
nearby places</string>
<key>NSLocationAlwaysUsageDescription</ke
y>
<string>We    need    your    location    to    show
nearby places</string>
```

Step 3: Get User Location

You can use the **geolocator** package to fetch the current location of the user. Here's how to do it:

```dart
import 'package:geolocator/geolocator.dart';

Future<void> getCurrentLocation() async {
  // Check if location services are enabled
  bool        serviceEnabled        =        await
Geolocator.isLocationServiceEnabled();
  if (!serviceEnabled) {
    // Location services are not enabled, request
the user to enable them
    print('Location services are disabled.');
    return;
  }
```

```
  // Request permissions to access location
  LocationPermission     permission     =     await
Geolocator.requestPermission();
  if (permission == LocationPermission.denied ||
permission == LocationPermission.deniedForever)
{
    // Permission denied, notify the user
    print('Location permission denied');
    return;
  }

  // Get the current location
  Position          position        =          await
Geolocator.getCurrentPosition(
    desiredAccuracy: LocationAccuracy.high,
  );
  print('Current position: ${position.latitude},
${position.longitude}');
}
```

In this code:

- **Geolocator.isLocationServiceEnabled()** checks if the location services are enabled on the device.
- **Geolocator.requestPermission()** asks the user for location permissions.
- **Geolocator.getCurrentPosition()** fetches the device's current latitude and longitude.

Step 4: Handling Location Changes

To track the user's location continuously, you can use **getPositionStream()** to listen for location updates.

```dart
StreamSubscription<Position> positionStream;

void startTrackingLocation() {
  positionStream = Geolocator.getPositionStream(
    locationSettings: LocationSettings(
      accuracy: LocationAccuracy.high,
      distanceFilter: 10,  // Updates every 10 meters
    ),
  ).listen((Position position) {
    print('Updated                     position:
${position.latitude}, ${position.longitude}');
  });
}
```

In this code, the app listens for updates every 10 meters and prints the updated position.

Displaying Maps with the google_maps_flutter Plugin

To display maps, Flutter provides the **google_maps_flutter** package, which integrates Google Maps into your app.

Step 1: Set Up Google Maps API Key

To use Google Maps, you must enable the **Google Maps API** and get an API key.

1. Go to the Google Cloud Console.
2. Create a new project or select an existing one.
3. Navigate to the **API & Services** > **Library** and search for **Google Maps SDK for Android** and **Google Maps SDK for iOS**.
4. Enable both APIs.
5. Go to **Credentials** and generate an API key.

Step 2: Add the API Key to Your Project

- **For Android**: In the android/app/src/main/AndroidManifest.xml file, add the following inside the <application> tag:

```xml

<meta-data
```

```
android:name="com.google.android.geo.API_
KEY"

android:value="YOUR_GOOGLE_MAPS_API_KEY"/
>
```

- **For iOS**: In the `ios/Runner/Info.plist` file, add the following:

xml

```
<key>IOSTransportSecurity</key>
<dict>
  <key>NSAppTransportSecurity</key>
  <dict>
    <key>NSAllowsArbitraryLoads</key>
    <true/>
  </dict>
</dict>
<key>NSLocationWhenInUseUsageDescription<
/key>
<string>We need your location to show the
map</string>
```

Step 3: Display Google Map

Now, you can display Google Maps in your app using the **GoogleMap** widget.

```dart
dart

import
'package:google_maps_flutter/google_maps_flutte
r.dart';
import 'package:flutter/material.dart';

class MapScreen extends StatefulWidget {
  @override
  _MapScreenState        createState()        =>
_MapScreenState();
}

class _MapScreenState extends State<MapScreen> {
  late GoogleMapController mapController;

  final      LatLng      _initialPosition      =
LatLng(37.7749,  -122.4194);   //  Example:  San
Francisco

  void           _onMapCreated(GoogleMapController
controller) {
    mapController = controller;
  }

  @override
  Widget build(BuildContext context) {
    return Scaffold(
```

```
    appBar:      AppBar(title:      Text('Google
Maps')),
      body: GoogleMap(
        onMapCreated: _onMapCreated,
        initialCameraPosition: CameraPosition(
          target: _initialPosition,
          zoom: 12,
        ),
        markers: {
          Marker(
            markerId: MarkerId('1'),
            position: _initialPosition,
            infoWindow:  InfoWindow(title:  'San
Francisco'),
          ),
        },
      ),
    );
  }
}
```

In this example:

- **GoogleMap** widget displays the map.
- **initialCameraPosition** sets the initial map position and zoom level.
- **Marker** adds a pin to the map at the specified position.

Step 4: Handling Map Interactions

You can interact with the map, such as moving the camera or adding markers, by using the `mapController`.

```dart

void _moveCamera() {

mapController.animateCamera(CameraUpdate.newCameraPosition(
    CameraPosition(target:    LatLng(34.0522,    -118.2437), zoom: 14),  // Move to LA
  ));
}
```

Example: Building a Location-Based App with a Map Interface

Let's build a simple **location-based app** where users can see their current location on a map and place a marker on it.

Step 1: Get User Location

We'll start by getting the user's current location using the **geolocator** package:

```dart

Position? _currentPosition;
```

```dart
Future<void> _getCurrentLocation() async {
  _currentPosition                =                await
Geolocator.getCurrentPosition(
    desiredAccuracy: LocationAccuracy.high,
  );
  setState(() {});
}
```

Step 2: Show User Location on the Map

We'll display the user's location on the map as a marker.

dart

```dart
GoogleMap(
  onMapCreated: _onMapCreated,
  initialCameraPosition: CameraPosition(
    target: _currentPosition != null
        ?    LatLng(_currentPosition!.latitude,
_currentPosition!.longitude)
        : LatLng(37.7749, -122.4194),
    zoom: 14,
  ),
  markers: {
    if (_currentPosition != null)
      Marker(
        markerId: MarkerId('userLocation'),
```

```
        position:
LatLng(_currentPosition!.latitude,
_currentPosition!.longitude),
        infoWindow:    InfoWindow(title:    'Your
Location'),
        ),
    },
)
```

Step 3: Add a Button to Get Current Location

You can add a button that fetches the current location and updates the map:

dart

```
ElevatedButton(
  onPressed: _getCurrentLocation,
  child: Text('Get My Location'),
)
```

When the user presses the button, it will update the map to show their current location.

Summary

In this chapter, we covered:

- **Using location services** with the `geolocator` package to get the user's current location and track location changes.
- **Displaying maps** using the `google_maps_flutter` plugin to show interactive maps with markers and camera control.
- A **real-world example** of building a location-based app with a map interface that shows the user's current location and allows them to place markers on the map.

By integrating geolocation and maps into your Flutter app, you can build location-based services that enhance user engagement and provide real-time location tracking.

CHAPTER 17

FLUTTER FOR WEB AND DESKTOP

In this chapter, we will explore **Flutter for Web** and **Flutter Desktop**, both of which allow you to expand your Flutter app beyond mobile platforms. Flutter provides a unified development experience for building applications for web, desktop, and mobile, all using the same codebase. We will discuss the benefits, challenges, and how to create a responsive web app and desktop applications for **macOS**, **Linux**, and **Windows** using Flutter. Finally, we will walk through a real-world example of creating a simple **Flutter web app**.

Flutter for Web: Benefits and Challenges

Benefits of Flutter for Web

1. **Single Codebase for Multiple Platforms**:
   o One of the key benefits of using Flutter for Web is the ability to use the same codebase for mobile, web, and desktop applications. This drastically reduces development time and effort as you don't have to maintain multiple codebases.

2. **Fast Development and Hot Reload**:

   o Just like on mobile, Flutter for Web offers the **hot reload** feature. This allows you to instantly view changes in your code without refreshing the entire app, which speeds up the development process.

3. **Performance**:

   o Flutter compiles directly to native machine code, and for the web, it uses **Dart's JIT (Just-In-Time) compilation**. While web support is still evolving, Flutter provides good performance for most use cases.

4. **Rich UI Components**:

   o Flutter provides a rich set of pre-built widgets that ensure consistency across mobile, web, and desktop platforms. You can also create custom widgets for more flexibility.

5. **Unified Design Language**:

   o Flutter provides consistent designs across platforms, including **Material Design** for Android, **Cupertino** for iOS, and responsive web designs for browsers.

Challenges of Flutter for Web

1. **Browser Compatibility**:

o Since Flutter is still in its early stages of web support, there may be some limitations or compatibility issues with older web browsers. Flutter supports modern browsers like Chrome, Firefox, Safari, and Edge, but performance and feature support can vary across browsers.

2. **Size and Performance**:

o Web applications built with Flutter can have larger bundle sizes compared to traditional web apps, which may affect loading times. Optimization techniques like **tree shaking** can help, but performance might still be a concern for more complex apps.

3. **Limited Access to Some Web-Specific Features**:

o Flutter for Web doesn't have native access to all web-specific APIs (such as specific browser features, or low-level access to browser rendering) and could have some limitations in terms of web performance compared to a dedicated JavaScript/HTML approach.

Building Responsive Web Apps with Flutter

Building responsive web apps means ensuring that your app adjusts its layout and design based on the size of the screen (whether desktop, tablet, or mobile).

Step 1: Use MediaQuery for Screen Size

Flutter provides **MediaQuery**, a widget that provides information about the screen size and orientation. You can use it to build a responsive UI that adapts to different screen sizes.

dart

```dart
class MyResponsiveApp extends StatelessWidget {
  @override
  Widget build(BuildContext context) {
    double width = MediaQuery.of(context).size.width;

    if (width > 800) {
      return Scaffold(body: Center(child: Text("Desktop View")));
    } else {
      return Scaffold(body: Center(child: Text("Mobile View")));
    }
  }
}
```

In this example:

- If the screen width is larger than 800 pixels (which is typical for desktop), we display a layout suitable for desktop.

- For smaller screen sizes, we show a mobile-friendly layout.

Step 2: Use LayoutBuilder for Flexibility

Flutter's **LayoutBuilder** widget provides a way to adjust the layout dynamically based on the available screen size or parent widget constraints. You can use it to build highly flexible and adaptive layouts.

dart

```
LayoutBuilder(
  builder: (context, constraints) {
    if (constraints.maxWidth > 800) {
      return DesktopLayout();
    } else {
      return MobileLayout();
    }
  },
)
```

The LayoutBuilder listens to changes in the parent's size, allowing for a more granular control over the UI.

Step 3: Implementing Responsive Widgets

You can use Flutter's built-in **Flexible**, **Expanded**, and **MediaQuery** widgets to create responsive designs that scale

231

properly across different screen sizes. This makes it easier to build apps that work on a variety of devices.

Flutter Desktop: macOS, Linux, and Windows Support

Flutter also extends its capabilities to **desktop apps** (macOS, Windows, and Linux). While mobile and web have been the primary focus of Flutter, desktop support is gaining momentum, and it's a great way to create cross-platform apps with Flutter.

Step 1: Setting Up Flutter Desktop

To build desktop apps with Flutter, ensure that your Flutter SDK is set up to support desktop development.

1. **Enable Desktop Support**: Ensure you are using the stable version of Flutter and enable desktop support using:

   bash

   ```
   flutter config --enable-macos-desktop
   flutter config --enable-linux-desktop
   flutter config --enable-windows-desktop
   ```

2. **Create a Desktop App**: When creating a new Flutter project, you can specify a target platform:

   bash

```
flutter create my_desktop_app
```

This will create a Flutter app with the necessary configuration files for macOS, Linux, and Windows.

3. **Run the App on Desktop**: Once you've created the app, you can run it on the desktop platform of your choice by using the following command:

```
bash
```

```
flutter run -d macos    # For macOS
flutter run -d linux    # For Linux
flutter run -d windows  # For Windows
```

Step 2: Building Desktop-Specific UIs

While Flutter's core widgets are available on desktop, you may want to build a desktop-specific UI using **desktop-friendly widgets**. For instance, you might want to use `TextField` with more desktop-specific features like multi-line editing, or use **custom windows** and **menus** that are common on desktop applications.

Example: Creating a Simple Flutter Web App

Now that we've covered the theory and setup, let's build a simple **Flutter web app** that displays a responsive layout and fetches data from an API.

Step 1: Set Up the Flutter Web Project

Create a new Flutter project with web support:

```bash
bash
```

```
flutter create flutter_web_app
cd flutter_web_app
```

This creates a basic Flutter app that you can run on both mobile and web.

Step 2: Create a Responsive Layout

Modify the `lib/main.dart` file to implement a responsive design using `MediaQuery` and `LayoutBuilder`:

```dart
dart
```

```dart
import 'package:flutter/material.dart';

void main() => runApp(MyApp());
```

```
class MyApp extends StatelessWidget {
  @override
  Widget build(BuildContext context) {
    return MaterialApp(
      home: HomeScreen(),
    );
  }
}


class HomeScreen extends StatelessWidget {
  @override
  Widget build(BuildContext context) {
    double           width           =
MediaQuery.of(context).size.width;

    return Scaffold(
      appBar: AppBar(title: Text("Flutter  Web
App")),
      body: Center(
        child: width > 600
            ? DesktopLayout()
            : MobileLayout(),
      ),
    );
  }
}


class DesktopLayout extends StatelessWidget {
  @override
```

```
Widget build(BuildContext context) {
  return Column(
    mainAxisAlignment:
MainAxisAlignment.center,
      children: [
        Text("Welcome to Desktop Layout", style:
TextStyle(fontSize: 24)),
        SizedBox(height: 20),
        ElevatedButton(
          onPressed: () {},
          child: Text("Click Me"),
        ),
      ],
    );
  }
}

class MobileLayout extends StatelessWidget {
  @override
  Widget build(BuildContext context) {
    return Column(
      mainAxisAlignment:
MainAxisAlignment.center,
        children: [
          Text("Welcome to Mobile Layout", style:
TextStyle(fontSize: 18)),
          SizedBox(height: 20),
          ElevatedButton(
            onPressed: () {},
```

```
        child: Text("Click Me"),
      ),
    ],
  );
}
}
```

In this example:

- We check the screen width using `MediaQuery` and display different layouts for desktop and mobile.
- The `DesktopLayout` has a larger font size and a simple button.
- The `MobileLayout` is more compact with a smaller font size.

Step 3: Fetch Data from an API (Optional)

To make the app dynamic, you can add a simple HTTP request to fetch data from an API and display it in the app.

Add the `http` package in the `pubspec.yaml` file:

```yaml
yaml

dependencies:
  http: ^0.14.0
```

Then, modify the `HomeScreen` widget to fetch and display data from an API:

dart

```dart
import 'dart:convert';
import 'package:http/http.dart' as http;

class HomeScreen extends StatelessWidget {
  Future<List<String>> fetchData() async {
    final response = await
http.get(Uri.parse('https://jsonplaceholder.typ
icode.com/posts'));
    if (response.statusCode == 200) {
      List<dynamic> data =
json.decode(response.body);
      return data.map((e) => e['title'] as
String).toList();
    } else {
      throw Exception('Failed to load data');
    }
  }

  @override
  Widget build(BuildContext context) {
    return Scaffold(
      appBar: AppBar(title: Text("Flutter Web
App")),
      body: FutureBuilder<List<String>>(
```

```
        future: fetchData(),
        builder: (context, snapshot) {
          if      (snapshot.connectionState    ==
ConnectionState.waiting) {
            return                 Center(child:
CircularProgressIndicator());
          } else if (snapshot.hasError) {
            return  Center(child:  Text('Error:
${snapshot.error}'));
          }   else   if   (!snapshot.hasData   ||
snapshot.data!.isEmpty) {
            return  Center(child:  Text('No  data
found'));
          }

          return ListView.builder(
            itemCount: snapshot.data!.length,
            itemBuilder: (context, index) {
              return              ListTile(title:
Text(snapshot.data![index]));
            },
          );
        },
      ),
    );
  }
}
```

This example fetches data from the **JSONPlaceholder** API and displays a list of titles in the app.

Summary

In this chapter, we explored:

- **Flutter for Web**: The benefits of using Flutter for web development, including a single codebase for mobile, web, and desktop.
- **Responsive design**: How to use `MediaQuery` and `LayoutBuilder` to create adaptive layouts that work across different screen sizes.
- **Flutter for Desktop**: Building apps for macOS, Linux, and Windows with Flutter, including setting up the environment and creating cross-platform desktop apps.
- A **real-world example** of creating a simple **Flutter web app** that fetches data from an API and displays it in a responsive layout.

Flutter is a powerful framework that allows you to target multiple platforms using a single codebase, making it easier to build apps for mobile, web, and desktop.

CHAPTER 18

TESTING IN FLUTTER – ENSURING QUALITY

In this chapter, we will explore **testing** in Flutter, focusing on ensuring the quality and reliability of your app through different types of tests. We'll cover **unit testing**, **widget testing**, and **integration testing**, providing practical examples and tips to help you write effective tests for your Flutter app. We will also walk through an example of writing tests for a **shopping cart app**.

Unit Testing in Flutter

Unit testing is the process of testing individual functions, methods, or classes to verify that each part of the app behaves as expected. Unit tests help ensure that the logic of your app is correct, independent of any UI components.

Step 1: Setting Up Unit Testing

Flutter provides the **test** package for writing unit tests. To add it to your project, include the following dependency in your `pubspec.yaml` file:

yaml

```yaml
dev_dependencies:
  test: ^1.16.0
```

Then, run `flutter pub get` to install the dependency.

Step 2: Writing a Simple Unit Test

Here's an example of a simple unit test for a function that calculates the total price of items in a shopping cart.

dart

```dart
// cart.dart
int calculateTotalPrice(List<int> itemPrices) {
  return itemPrices.fold(0, (total, price) =>
total + price);
}
```

Now, let's write a unit test for this function:

dart

```dart
import 'package:test/test.dart';
import 'cart.dart';

void main() {
  group('Shopping Cart', () {
```

```
test('calculates total price correctly', ()
{
    final itemPrices = [100, 200, 50];
    final            total            =
calculateTotalPrice(itemPrices);
    expect(total, 350);
  });

  test('returns 0 for an empty cart', () {
    final itemPrices = [];
    final            total            =
calculateTotalPrice(itemPrices);
    expect(total, 0);
  });
  });
}
```

In this test:

- We use **group** to group related tests.
- The **test** function defines individual test cases.
- We use the **expect** function to assert that the result matches the expected value.

Step 3: Running Unit Tests

You can run your unit tests with the following command:

```bash
bash
```

```
flutter test
```

This command will run all the tests in the `test` directory.

Widget Testing: Testing UI Components

Widget testing focuses on testing individual widgets or UI components. Flutter provides the **flutter_test** package for testing widgets. This type of testing is useful for checking the behavior of widgets and their interaction with other widgets.

Step 1: Setting Up Widget Testing

Widget testing is already included in Flutter projects. You do not need to add a separate dependency, as **flutter_test** comes bundled with Flutter.

Step 2: Writing a Simple Widget Test

Let's test a simple **ShoppingCartWidget** that displays the total price of items in the shopping cart.

```dart

// shopping_cart_widget.dart
import 'package:flutter/material.dart';
```

```dart
class ShoppingCartWidget extends StatelessWidget
{
  final List<int> itemPrices;

  ShoppingCartWidget({required
this.itemPrices});

  int calculateTotalPrice() {
    return itemPrices.fold(0, (total, price) =>
total + price);
  }

  @override
  Widget build(BuildContext context) {
    return Column(
      children: [
        Text('Total:
\$$${calculateTotalPrice()}'),
      ],
    );
  }
}
```

Now, let's write a widget test for this component:

dart

```dart
import 'package:flutter/material.dart';
import 'package:flutter_test/flutter_test.dart';
import 'shopping_cart_widget.dart';
```

```
void main() {
    testWidgets('ShoppingCartWidget shows correct
total', (WidgetTester tester) async {
        // Build the widget tree.
        await tester.pumpWidget(MaterialApp(
            home:                         Scaffold(body:
ShoppingCartWidget(itemPrices: [100, 200, 50]))),
        ));

        // Find the Text widget and check its value.
        final    textFinder    =    find.text('Total:
\$350');
        expect(textFinder, findsOneWidget);
    });

    testWidgets('ShoppingCartWidget shows 0 for an
empty cart', (WidgetTester tester) async {
        // Build the widget tree with an empty cart.
        await tester.pumpWidget(MaterialApp(
            home:                         Scaffold(body:
ShoppingCartWidget(itemPrices: [])),
        ));

        // Find the Text widget and check its value.
        final textFinder = find.text('Total: \$0');
        expect(textFinder, findsOneWidget);
    });
}
```

In this test:

- **testWidgets** is used to define the widget test.
- **tester.pumpWidget** builds the widget tree in the test environment.
- **find.text** is used to locate the Text widget with the expected content.
- **expect** is used to verify that the correct value is displayed.

Step 3: Running Widget Tests

You can run your widget tests using the following command:

```bash

flutter test
```

Integration Testing: End-to-End Testing

Integration testing checks the overall functionality of the app, ensuring that different components work together as expected. This type of testing simulates real user interactions and verifies that the app behaves correctly from start to finish.

Step 1: Set Up Integration Testing

Flutter provides the **integration_test** package for end-to-end testing. To set it up, add the following dependency to your `pubspec.yaml` file:

yaml

```yaml
dev_dependencies:
  integration_test: ^2.0.0
  flutter_driver: ^0.0.0
```

Also, add the following import to your `main.dart`:

dart

```dart
import
'package:integration_test/integration_test.dart
';
```

Step 2: Writing an Integration Test

Let's write an integration test for a shopping cart app that adds an item and checks the total price:

dart

```dart
import
'package:integration_test/integration_test.dart
';
```

```
import 'package:flutter/material.dart';
import 'package:flutter_test/flutter_test.dart';
import 'shopping_cart_widget.dart';

void main() {

IntegrationTestWidgetsFlutterBinding.ensureInit
ialized();

  testWidgets('Add item to cart and check total',
(WidgetTester tester) async {
    // Build the app.
    await tester.pumpWidget(MaterialApp(
      home:                     Scaffold(body:
ShoppingCartWidget(itemPrices: [100]))),
    ));

    // Verify initial total is 100.
    expect(find.text('Total:            \$100'),
findsOneWidget);

    // Add another item.
    await tester.pumpWidget(MaterialApp(
      home:                     Scaffold(body:
ShoppingCartWidget(itemPrices: [100, 200]))),
    ));

    // Verify updated total is 300.
```

249

```
    expect(find.text('Total:              \$300'),
findsOneWidget);
  });
}
```

In this example:

- **IntegrationTestWidgetsFlutterBinding.ensu reInitialized()** ensures that integration testing is properly set up.
- **testWidgets** runs the test, verifying that the app behaves as expected when an item is added to the cart.

Step 3: Running Integration Tests

To run integration tests, you can use the following command:

```
bash
```

```
flutter test integration_test/app_test.dart
```

Example: Writing Tests for a Shopping Cart App

Now that we've covered unit, widget, and integration tests, let's go through a complete example of testing a **shopping cart app**. We will write unit tests for the cart calculation logic, widget tests for the UI components, and integration tests for the overall user flow.

1. **Unit Test**: Verify that the cart calculation logic correctly sums up the prices.
2. **Widget Test**: Verify that the UI correctly updates when the user adds or removes items from the cart.
3. **Integration Test**: Simulate a user adding items to the cart and check if the total is correctly updated.

By writing comprehensive tests, you ensure that your app behaves as expected across all platforms and scenarios.

Summary

In this chapter, we covered:

- **Unit testing**: Testing individual functions and logic in isolation.
- **Widget testing**: Testing individual UI components to ensure correct behavior and layout.
- **Integration testing**: End-to-end testing to ensure that the app's components work together properly and simulate real user interactions.
- A **real-world example** of writing tests for a **shopping cart app**, covering all three types of tests.

By incorporating testing into your Flutter development workflow, you can ensure that your app remains reliable, maintainable, and high-quality as it evolves. Testing allows you to catch bugs early, reduce regressions, and ensure a smooth user experience.

CHAPTER 19

DEBUGGING AND PERFORMANCE OPTIMIZATION

In this chapter, we will dive into **debugging** and **performance optimization** in Flutter. While building apps, it is essential to ensure that they run efficiently and are free of bugs. We'll cover how to use **Flutter DevTools** to debug your app, analyze its performance and memory usage, and optimize your Flutter app for better performance. We will also walk through a **real-world example** of improving the performance of a **ListView app**.

Using Flutter DevTools for Debugging

Flutter DevTools is a suite of debugging tools that provide insights into the performance and behavior of your Flutter app. It helps with debugging, profiling, and tracking performance issues like slow frames, memory leaks, and inefficient rendering.

Step 1: Installing Flutter DevTools

1. First, make sure you have **Flutter** and **Dart SDK** installed, as well as **Android Studio** or **Visual Studio Code** as your IDE.

2. Flutter DevTools is already included in the Flutter SDK, so you don't need to install anything separately.

Step 2: Launching Flutter DevTools

To launch **DevTools**:

1. **From Android Studio**:
   o Open your Flutter project in Android Studio.
   o Run the app using the **Run** or **Debug** button.
   o Click on the **Flutter DevTools** icon (a small bug icon) in the top-right corner of Android Studio.

2. **From VS Code**:
   o Open your Flutter project in VS Code.
   o Use the **Run** or **Debug** command (F5) to launch the app.
   o In the debug panel, click on **Open DevTools**.

Alternatively, you can launch DevTools from the command line by running:

bash

```
flutter pub global activate devtools
flutter pub global run devtools
```

This will start the DevTools server and open the web-based UI in your browser.

Step 3: Using the DevTools Features

DevTools provides a variety of useful features for debugging and profiling your app:

- **Inspector**: This tool allows you to inspect the widget tree of your app, view the properties of individual widgets, and identify any issues with widget rendering.
- **Timeline**: The timeline shows the performance of your app, including frame rendering times and CPU usage, so you can spot bottlenecks.
- **Memory**: This tool helps you monitor memory usage, track memory leaks, and manage objects that take up a lot of memory.
- **CPU Profiler**: This shows CPU usage over time, helping you detect performance issues related to inefficient code or expensive operations.

Step 4: Debugging with Breakpoints and Logging

In addition to DevTools, you can use **breakpoints** and **logging** to debug your Flutter app:

- **Breakpoints**: Set breakpoints in your code to pause execution and inspect variable values. In **Android Studio** or **VS Code**, click on the line number where you want to set the breakpoint, and the app will pause there during debugging.

- **Logging**: Use `print()` statements to log information to the console for debugging purposes.

Example:

dart

```
void addToCart(int price) {
  print('Adding item with price: $price');
  cart.add(price);
}
```

Analyzing App Performance and Memory Usage

Flutter provides tools to analyze your app's **performance** and **memory usage**, which are critical for optimizing app speed and reducing resource consumption.

Step 1: Analyzing Performance with DevTools

To track the performance of your Flutter app, use the **Timeline** feature in DevTools. It provides insights into:

- **Frame rendering times**: Each frame of the app is rendered at 60 FPS by default. If frames take too long to render, it can lead to janky animations and poor user experience.

- **CPU usage**: Monitor the CPU usage to identify which parts of your app are consuming the most processing power.

- **Widget rebuild times**: Identify inefficient widgets that are rebuilt too frequently.

Step 2: Analyzing Memory Usage

In DevTools, the **Memory** tab helps you monitor your app's memory usage over time. You can check for:

- **Memory leaks**: If your app holds onto memory unnecessarily, it can eventually lead to crashes or poor performance. Use DevTools to track memory allocations and identify any leaks.

- **Object allocation**: The memory tool also shows the number of objects allocated during runtime, helping you identify if certain objects are consuming too much memory.

Step 3: Identifying and Fixing Performance Bottlenecks

Common performance bottlenecks include:

- **Expensive computations on the main thread**: If your app is performing heavy calculations on the main thread, it can block the UI and cause jank.

- **Large widget trees**: If you have many widgets on the screen, it can slow down rendering and lead to high CPU usage.
- **Unnecessary rebuilds**: Widgets that rebuild too often can reduce app performance. Using **const constructors** and **shouldRebuild()** can help avoid unnecessary rebuilds.

Optimizing Flutter Apps for Better Performance

Performance optimization is key to providing a smooth user experience. Here are a few strategies to optimize your Flutter apps:

1. Reduce Widget Rebuilds

Flutter rebuilds widgets when their state changes. However, unnecessary rebuilds can cause performance issues. To optimize this:

- Use **const constructors** for widgets that do not change.
- Use **StatefulWidget** only when necessary. For static widgets, prefer **StatelessWidget**.
- Use **ValueListenableBuilder** and **StreamBuilder** to listen to changes in specific data rather than rebuilding entire widget trees.

2. Optimize Images and Assets

Large images can slow down your app, especially if they are loaded into memory inefficiently. Here are some strategies:

- Use **Image.asset** and **Image.network** wisely. Avoid loading large images into memory unless needed.
- For network images, use **cached_network_image** to cache images locally and reduce network requests.
- Compress images to reduce their size without compromising quality.

3. Avoid Expensive Operations on the Main Thread

Heavy operations, like **file I/O**, **network requests**, or **database queries**, should be offloaded to separate threads to avoid blocking the UI. You can use **Isolates** or **Future.delayed** to perform such operations asynchronously.

4. Use Lazy Loading for Large Lists

When dealing with large lists (e.g., in a **ListView**), avoid loading all items at once. Instead, use **lazy loading** to load items as the user scrolls. The **ListView.builder** constructor is useful for building large lists efficiently.

Example:

```dart
ListView.builder(
  itemCount: items.length,
  itemBuilder: (context, index) {
    return ListTile(
      title: Text(items[index]),
    );
  },
)
```

5. Use the `flutter_driver` for Performance Testing

Use the **flutter_driver** package to test the performance of your Flutter app, especially for interactions and animations. This helps identify performance bottlenecks in user flows and animation transitions.

Example: Improving the Performance of a ListView App

Let's walk through an example of optimizing the performance of a **ListView app** that displays a large number of items.

Step 1: Initial Code with Performance Issues

Consider an app where we display a list of 1000 items without optimization. Here's how the code might look:

```dart
```

```
ListView(
  children: List.generate(1000, (index) {
    return ListTile(
      title: Text('Item $index'),
    );
  }),
)
```

This approach results in all 1000 items being built in memory at once, which can cause high memory usage and slow performance.

Step 2: Optimized Code Using `ListView.builder`

To optimize, we can use **ListView.builder**, which lazily loads items as the user scrolls. This reduces memory usage and improves performance:

dart

```
ListView.builder(
  itemCount: 1000,
  itemBuilder: (context, index) {
    return ListTile(
      title: Text('Item $index'),
    );
  },
)
```

Now, only the visible items are built, and items outside of the viewport are disposed of when they are no longer needed, significantly improving performance.

Step 3: Further Optimization Using `const` Widgets

If the content of the items doesn't change dynamically, you can make the `ListTile` widget **const**:

dart

```
ListView.builder(
  itemCount: 1000,
  itemBuilder: (context, index) {
    return const ListTile(
      title: Text('Item'),
    );
  },
)
```

This reduces rebuild costs and optimizes performance even further.

Summary

In this chapter, we covered:

- **Flutter DevTools** for debugging, profiling, and analyzing app performance and memory usage.
- How to use **DevTools** to debug your app and track performance issues, such as frame rendering times and CPU usage.
- Strategies to **optimize Flutter apps** for better performance, including reducing widget rebuilds, optimizing images, and avoiding heavy operations on the main thread.
- A **real-world example** of improving the performance of a **ListView app** by using **lazy loading** and `const` **widgets**.

By following these techniques, you can ensure that your Flutter apps are efficient, responsive, and provide a smooth user experience, even when dealing with complex layouts or large data sets.

CHAPTER 20

CUSTOMIZING FLUTTER WIDGETS AND THEMES

In this chapter, we will explore how to create custom widgets and reusable components, and how to customize the appearance of your Flutter app using **themes**. Custom widgets are essential for maintaining consistency across your app and simplifying the development process. By using Flutter's theming capabilities, you can create a cohesive and visually appealing design. We'll also walk through an example of building a **custom button** and **theme** for your app.

Creating Custom Widgets

In Flutter, **custom widgets** allow you to build complex UI components that can be reused across different parts of your app. Custom widgets are built by composing smaller widgets and encapsulating them into one reusable unit.

Step 1: Basic Custom Widget

A custom widget is simply a class that extends **StatelessWidget** or **StatefulWidget**. Let's start by creating a simple custom widget that displays a card with a title and description:

dart

```dart
import 'package:flutter/material.dart';

class CustomCard extends StatelessWidget {
  final String title;
  final String description;

  CustomCard({required    this.title,    required
this.description});

  @override
  Widget build(BuildContext context) {
    return Card(
      elevation: 5.0,
      margin: EdgeInsets.all(10.0),
      child: Padding(
        padding: EdgeInsets.all(16.0),
        child: Column(
          crossAxisAlignment:
CrossAxisAlignment.start,
          children: [
            Text(title,                    style:
Theme.of(context).textTheme.headline6),
            SizedBox(height: 8.0),
```

```
        Text(description,              style:
Theme.of(context).textTheme.bodyText2),
          ],
        ),
      ),
    );
  }
}
```

In this example:

- **CustomCard** is a custom stateless widget.
- We pass **title** and **description** as parameters to customize the widget.
- Inside the `build()` method, we use Flutter's built-in **Card** widget and **Text** widgets to display the content.

Step 2: Using the Custom Widget

To use the custom widget in your app, simply instantiate it where needed:

dart

```
class HomePage extends StatelessWidget {
  @override
  Widget build(BuildContext context) {
    return Scaffold(
```

266

```
      appBar:      AppBar(title:      Text('Custom
Widgets')),
        body: ListView(
          children: [
            CustomCard(
              title: 'Custom Widget 1',
              description: 'This is a custom widget
with a title and description.',
            ),
            CustomCard(
              title: 'Custom Widget 2',
              description: 'Another example of a
reusable custom widget.',
            ),
          ],
        ),
      );
  }
}
```

In this case, we use **CustomCard** twice with different data, demonstrating how reusable custom widgets work in Flutter.

Building Reusable Components

Reusable components in Flutter can help you avoid duplication of code and make your app more modular and maintainable. Custom

267

widgets can be used to encapsulate common UI elements, like buttons, cards, headers, etc., that you use throughout your app.

Step 1: Reusable Custom Button

Let's create a reusable custom button widget that can be customized with different text and colors:

dart

```dart
class CustomButton extends StatelessWidget {
  final String label;
  final Color color;
  final VoidCallback onPressed;

  CustomButton({required this.label, required this.color, required this.onPressed});

  @override
  Widget build(BuildContext context) {
    return ElevatedButton(
      style: ElevatedButton.styleFrom(
        primary: color,
        padding: EdgeInsets.symmetric(vertical: 12.0, horizontal: 24.0),
        shape: RoundedRectangleBorder(
          borderRadius: BorderRadius.circular(8.0),
        ),
```

```
    ),
    onPressed: onPressed,
    child: Text(
      label,
      style: TextStyle(fontSize: 16.0, color:
Colors.white),
    ),
  );
  }
}
```

In this example:

- **CustomButton** is a stateless widget that takes **label**, **color**, and **onPressed** as parameters.
- **ElevatedButton.styleFrom** is used to customize the button's appearance, such as background color, padding, and border radius.
- The **onPressed** callback is used to handle button press events.

Step 2: Using the Custom Button

You can now use the CustomButton widget anywhere in your app with different labels and colors:

```
dart
```

```
CustomButton(
```

269

```
label: 'Press Me',
color: Colors.blue,
onPressed: () {
  print('Button Pressed!');
},
),
```

This approach makes your buttons reusable and customizable, reducing code duplication and improving maintainability.

Flutter Themes: Customizing App Appearance

Flutter's **theming** capabilities allow you to define consistent styles across your app. You can customize various visual elements like **colors**, **typography**, and **button styles** in one central place and apply them across the app.

Step 1: Defining a Custom Theme

To create a custom theme, you need to define a `ThemeData` object. The `ThemeData` class allows you to customize the app's appearance, such as the primary color, text styles, button themes, etc.

Here's how you can define a custom theme for your app:

```
dart
```

```
final ThemeData customTheme = ThemeData(
  primaryColor: Colors.blue,
  accentColor: Colors.orange,
  textTheme: TextTheme(
    headline6:  TextStyle(color:  Colors.black,
fontSize: 20.0, fontWeight: FontWeight.bold),
    bodyText2:                     TextStyle(color:
Colors.grey[600], fontSize: 16.0),
  ),
  buttonTheme: ButtonThemeData(
    buttonColor: Colors.blue,
    shape: RoundedRectangleBorder(
      borderRadius: BorderRadius.circular(8.0),
    ),
  ),
);
```

In this example:

- **primaryColor** defines the main color of the app.
- **accentColor** is used for UI elements like floating action buttons or highlighted text.
- **textTheme** defines the text styles for different parts of the app, like headlines and body text.
- **buttonTheme** customizes the appearance of buttons.

Step 2: Applying the Custom Theme

To apply the custom theme globally across your app, use the **Theme** widget in the root of your app:

dart

```dart
class MyApp extends StatelessWidget {
  @override
  Widget build(BuildContext context) {
    return MaterialApp(
      title: 'Custom Theme Example',
      theme: customTheme,  // Apply the custom theme
      home: HomePage(),
    );
  }
}
```

Now, all the widgets in the app will use the custom theme defined earlier, including buttons, text, and other UI components.

Example: Building a Custom Button and Theme for Your App

Let's combine the concepts of **custom widgets** and **themes** to create a **custom button** that uses the app's theme.

Step 1: Define a Custom Button that Uses the Theme

dart

```
class ThemedButton extends StatelessWidget {
  final String label;
  final VoidCallback onPressed;

  ThemedButton({required this.label, required this.onPressed});

  @override
  Widget build(BuildContext context) {
    final theme = Theme.of(context);  // Access the current theme

    return ElevatedButton(
      style: ElevatedButton.styleFrom(
        primary: theme.primaryColor,  // Use primary color from the theme
        padding: EdgeInsets.symmetric(vertical: 12.0, horizontal: 24.0),
        shape: RoundedRectangleBorder(
          borderRadius: BorderRadius.circular(8.0),
        ),
      ),
      onPressed: onPressed,
      child: Text(
        label,
```

```
      style:
theme.textTheme.bodyText2?.With(color:
Colors.white),   // Use body text style from the
theme
      ),
    );
  }
}
```

In this example:

- **ThemedButton** is a custom button widget that uses the **Theme.of(context)** method to access the app's current theme.
- The button's color and text style are derived from the theme, ensuring consistency across the app.

Step 2: Use the Themed Button in the App

Now, let's use the ThemedButton in a screen:

dart

```
class HomePage extends StatelessWidget {
  @override
  Widget build(BuildContext context) {
    return Scaffold(
      appBar: AppBar(title: Text('Custom Theme
Example')),
```

```
body: Center(
  child: ThemedButton(
    label: 'Press Me',
    onPressed: () {
      print('Button Pressed!');
    },
  ),
),
);
}
}
```

Here, the **ThemedButton** automatically uses the custom theme defined in the MaterialApp.

Summary

In this chapter, we covered:

- **Custom widgets** in Flutter, which allow you to build reusable UI components by composing smaller widgets.
- **Reusable components**, such as a custom button widget that can be customized with different labels, colors, and actions.
- **Flutter themes**, which allow you to define consistent styles (e.g., colors, typography, button styles) across your app.

- A **real-world example** of building a **custom button** and **theme** for your app to maintain consistent design.

Customizing widgets and themes in Flutter enables you to create a unified and maintainable user interface across your app, improving both development efficiency and user experience.

CHAPTER 21

ACCESSIBILITY IN FLUTTER – MAKING APPS INCLUSIVE

In this chapter, we will explore **accessibility** in Flutter, an important aspect of mobile app development that ensures your app is usable by people with disabilities. Accessibility makes your app **inclusive** by enabling users with various impairments, such as visual, auditory, and motor disabilities, to interact with your app effectively. We will cover why accessibility is crucial, how to use Flutter's accessibility features like **screen readers** and **color contrast**, and provide a **real-world example** of making a simple **form app accessible**.

Importance of Accessibility in Mobile Apps

Accessibility refers to the design and development of apps that can be used by individuals with various disabilities. In a mobile app, this can include features that help users with visual, auditory, cognitive, and motor impairments.

Why Accessibility Matters:

1. **Wider Audience**: Making your app accessible allows a larger audience, including individuals with disabilities, to use it.

2. **Legal and Ethical Responsibility**: Many countries have laws and regulations requiring apps to be accessible, such as the **Americans with Disabilities Act (ADA)** in the United States and **Web Content Accessibility Guidelines (WCAG)**. Additionally, making your app accessible is ethically important as it ensures equality for all users.

3. **Improved Usability**: Accessibility features improve the overall usability of the app. For example, better color contrast or support for screen readers benefits all users, not just those with disabilities.

Key Benefits of Accessibility:

- **Increased user engagement** from a broader demographic.
- **Better user experience** for individuals with different needs.
- **Compliance** with legal and regulatory requirements.

Using Accessibility Features in Flutter

Flutter provides built-in support for a variety of accessibility features that help make your apps more inclusive. These features are designed to help users with different disabilities interact with your app more easily. Let's look at some key Flutter accessibility features:

1. Screen Readers (TalkBack, VoiceOver)

A **screen reader** is a tool that reads out the content displayed on the screen to the user. Flutter supports **TalkBack** for Android and **VoiceOver** for iOS. These screen readers help users with visual impairments by reading out the UI elements on the screen.

To make your app compatible with screen readers, you can use the `semantics` widget in Flutter to provide descriptive text for UI elements.

Step 1: Adding Semantics to Widgets

You can wrap widgets like buttons, images, and other interactive elements with the `Semantics` widget to give them accessible labels.

```dart
Semantics(
```

```
label: 'Submit Button',
child: ElevatedButton(
  onPressed: () {},
  child: Text('Submit'),
),
)
```

In this example, the **Semantics** widget is used to label a button, making it accessible for screen readers. When the button is focused, the screen reader will announce **"Submit Button"** to the user.

2. Color Contrast and Visual Accessibility

For users with low vision or color blindness, **color contrast** is an important aspect of accessibility. To ensure your app is accessible to these users, use high contrast between background and text colors.

Step 1: Ensuring Proper Color Contrast

Flutter's **ThemeData** allows you to define color schemes that are optimized for accessibility. By choosing colors with sufficient contrast, you ensure that your text is readable for users with visual impairments.

Example:

```
dart
```

```
final ThemeData customTheme = ThemeData(
  primaryColor: Colors.blue,
  accentColor: Colors.orange,
  textTheme: TextTheme(
    bodyText2: TextStyle(color: Colors.black),
// High contrast for readability
  ),
  scaffoldBackgroundColor: Colors.white,
);
```

Ensure that the text color and background color provide sufficient contrast according to accessibility guidelines (WCAG). Tools like **Color Contrast Checker** can help you check whether the color combinations meet accessibility standards.

Step 2: Testing Color Contrast

You can use accessibility testing tools like **aXe** or **Color Contrast Analyzer** to evaluate the color contrast ratio of your app and make adjustments if needed.

3. Accessibility Actions and Navigation

Flutter provides ways to make actions like buttons and forms more accessible by supporting gestures and keyboard navigation. Using **focus** and **onTap** actions can help users with limited mobility interact with your app effectively.

281

Example of adding a focus action to a button:

dart

```
FocusableActionDetector(
  onShowFocusHighlight: (isFocused) {
    print('Button focused: $isFocused');
  },
  child: ElevatedButton(
    onPressed: () {},
    child: Text('Click Me'),
  ),
)
```

This widget helps focus on buttons and shows focus highlights when using keyboard navigation.

Example: Making a Form App Accessible

Let's walk through a simple example of making a **form app accessible** by ensuring that all form fields are readable by screen readers, have good color contrast, and are easy to navigate.

Step 1: Building a Simple Form

Here's a simple form with a text field and a submit button:

dart

```dart
import 'package:flutter/material.dart';

void main() {
  runApp(MyApp());
}

class MyApp extends StatelessWidget {
  @override
  Widget build(BuildContext context) {
    return MaterialApp(
      home: Scaffold(
        appBar: AppBar(title: Text('Accessible Form')),
        body: AccessibleForm(),
      ),
    );
  }
}

class AccessibleForm extends StatelessWidget {
  final TextEditingController _controller = TextEditingController();

  @override
  Widget build(BuildContext context) {
    return Padding(
      padding: const EdgeInsets.all(16.0),
      child: Column(
```

283

```
        crossAxisAlignment:
CrossAxisAlignment.start,
        children: [
          // Text field with a semantics label
for screen readers
          Semantics(
            label: 'Name input field',
            child: TextField(
              controller: _controller,
              decoration:
InputDecoration(labelText: 'Name'),
            ),
          ),
          SizedBox(height: 20),
          // Submit button with semantics for
screen readers
          Semantics(
            label: 'Submit button',
            child: ElevatedButton(
              onPressed: () {
                print('Name:
${_controller.text}');
              },
              child: Text('Submit'),
            ),
          ),
        ],
      ),
    );
```

```
    }
}
```

Step 2: Adding Accessibility Features

1. **Screen Reader Support**: We wrapped the `TextField` and `ElevatedButton` with the `Semantics` widget and added a label, so when the user focuses on these elements, the screen reader announces the labels to the user.

2. **High Contrast**: We're using the default Flutter theme, but you can customize it for better color contrast. Ensure the text and background colors are easy to read.

dart

```dart
final ThemeData customTheme = ThemeData(
  primaryColor: Colors.blue,
  accentColor: Colors.orange,
  textTheme: TextTheme(
    bodyText2: TextStyle(color: Colors.black),
// High contrast
  ),
  scaffoldBackgroundColor: Colors.white,
);
```

3. **Focus Management**: For a more advanced example, you can manage focus and keyboard navigation using `FocusNode` and `FocusableActionDetector` to

support users navigating the form using a keyboard or assistive technology.

Step 3: Testing Accessibility

Once you've added the necessary accessibility features, it's crucial to test your app for accessibility:

1. **Use Screen Reader Tools**: Enable **TalkBack** on Android or **VoiceOver** on iOS to test how your app behaves with screen readers.
2. **Test Color Contrast**: Use tools like **Color Contrast Analyzer** to ensure your app meets accessibility guidelines for color contrast.
3. **Keyboard and Gesture Navigation**: Test keyboard navigation and gestures to make sure the app is usable for users with motor impairments.

Summary

In this chapter, we explored the importance of **accessibility** in mobile apps and how to ensure your Flutter app is inclusive. Key topics included:

- **Accessibility in Flutter**: How to use Flutter's accessibility features like **screen readers, color contrast**, and **focus management**.

- **Customizing Widgets**: Making custom widgets accessible by adding semantics, proper labeling, and ensuring that all interactive elements are screen reader-friendly.

- **Example**: We built a simple **form app** and added accessibility features like **Semantics** for screen readers and high color contrast for better readability.

By implementing accessibility in your Flutter apps, you ensure that your app can be used by a wider audience, including individuals with disabilities, making it more inclusive and compliant with accessibility standards.

CHAPTER 22

ADVANCED STATE MANAGEMENT – PROVIDER, RIVERPOD, BLOC

State management is a crucial part of Flutter development, allowing you to control how data is passed between widgets and how UI updates are triggered. As Flutter apps grow in complexity, state management solutions become essential for maintaining clean, efficient, and maintainable code. In this chapter, we will dive into **advanced state management solutions** in Flutter, focusing on **Provider**, **Riverpod**, and **Bloc**. We'll explore their differences and use cases, with a detailed example of building a **movie app** using **Bloc** for state management.

Deep Dive into Advanced State Management Solutions

Flutter offers several solutions for managing state, ranging from simple to advanced approaches. The state management solution you choose depends on your app's complexity and the use case.

- **Provider**: A simple and flexible solution for dependency injection and state management. It's easy to use and understand, making it a great choice for small to medium-sized apps.

- **Riverpod**: An improved version of **Provider**, designed by the same author. Riverpod offers a more powerful, flexible, and testable state management approach. It addresses some limitations of **Provider** and simplifies testing and refactoring.

- **Bloc (Business Logic Component)**: A more complex state management solution for apps with heavy business logic. Bloc allows you to separate your app's UI from its business logic and provides fine-grained control over state transitions. It uses the **Streams** API to manage state, making it ideal for complex applications that require asynchronous data handling.

Provider vs. Riverpod vs. Bloc: Understanding the Differences

Each state management solution in Flutter has its strengths and weaknesses. Here's a breakdown of the differences between **Provider**, **Riverpod**, and **Bloc**:

1. Provider

- **Simplicity**: Provider is one of the simplest and most widely used state management solutions in Flutter.

- **Use Case**: Ideal for small to medium-sized apps or simple state management needs, such as global state or UI-related state.
- **Structure**: Uses `ChangeNotifier` and `Consumer` widgets to propagate state updates across the widget tree.
- **Pros**:
  - Easy to understand and implement.
  - Good for managing simple or app-wide state.
  - Integrated with Flutter's reactive model (widgets automatically rebuild when the state changes).
- **Cons**:
  - Lacks some advanced features available in Riverpod or Bloc.
  - Can become cumbersome as the app grows larger.

2. Riverpod

- **Simplicity**: Riverpod is a more powerful alternative to Provider, designed to address Provider's limitations.
- **Use Case**: Ideal for medium to large apps where you need more flexibility, improved testing, and better management of complex state.
- **Structure**: Riverpod uses **Providers** but does not require the `ChangeNotifier` or `Consumer` widget. It's designed to be more modular and testable.
- **Pros**:

o   Improved testing and flexibility compared to Provider.

o   No dependence on Flutter's widget tree, which makes it better suited for both Flutter and non-Flutter (Dart) apps.

o   Strong compile-time safety and better error handling.

- **Cons**:

   o   Slightly more complex than Provider, which might be overkill for small apps.

   o   Newer and less widely adopted than Provider.

3. Bloc

- **Simplicity**: Bloc is a more complex solution than Provider and Riverpod, designed for large-scale apps with complex business logic.

- **Use Case**: Ideal for apps that require advanced state management, asynchronous data handling, and clear separation of concerns (business logic vs. UI).

- **Structure**: Bloc uses **Streams** and **Sinks** to manage state. Business logic is decoupled from the UI, with **Events** triggering state transitions, and the **Bloc** emitting new states.

- **Pros**:

   o   Clear separation between business logic and UI code.

291

- o Better suited for complex, large-scale apps with asynchronous operations (e.g., API calls, real-time data).
- o Predictable state transitions using Streams and Events.

- **Cons**:

  - o Steeper learning curve compared to Provider and Riverpod.
  - o More boilerplate code, especially for managing state and events.

Using BLoC for Complex State Management

Bloc is a powerful state management solution that makes it easy to handle complex state transitions. It helps separate the UI from the business logic, making the code more maintainable and scalable. In a typical **BLoC** architecture, you will have:

1. **Events**: Represent the actions that trigger a change in the state (e.g., button presses, API responses).
2. **States**: Represent the different states your app can be in (e.g., loading, loaded, error).
3. **Bloc**: The central class that processes **Events** and outputs **States**.

Step 1: Setting Up Bloc

To get started with Bloc, you need to add the following dependencies to your `pubspec.yaml` file:

yaml

```yaml
dependencies:
  flutter_bloc: ^8.0.1
  bloc: ^8.0.1
```

After adding the dependencies, run `flutter pub get` to install them.

Step 2: Building a Movie App with Bloc

Let's build a simple **movie app** that displays a list of movies. The app will fetch data from a mock API (for simplicity) and display the movies in a `ListView`. We will use **Bloc** for state management.

1. **Define the States and Events**

First, we define the **states** and **events** for the app:

dart

```dart
// movie_event.dart
abstract class MovieEvent {}
```

```dart
class FetchMovies extends MovieEvent {}

// movie_state.dart
abstract class MovieState {}

class MoviesInitial extends MovieState {}

class MoviesLoading extends MovieState {}

class MoviesLoaded extends MovieState {
  final List<String> movies;

  MoviesLoaded({required this.movies});
}

class MoviesError extends MovieState {
  final String message;

  MoviesError({required this.message});
}
```

Here:

- **FetchMovies** is an event that triggers the movie fetch operation.
- The states include:
  - **MoviesLoading**: When movies are being fetched.

294

- o **MoviesLoaded**: When movies are successfully loaded.
- o **MoviesError**: When an error occurs while fetching movies.

2. **Create the Bloc**

Next, we create the **MovieBloc** that processes the events and yields the appropriate states:

dart

```
// movie_bloc.dart
import 'dart:async';
import 'package:bloc/bloc.dart';
import 'movie_event.dart';
import 'movie_state.dart';

class MovieBloc extends Bloc<MovieEvent,
MovieState> {
  MovieBloc() : super(MoviesInitial());

  @override
  Stream<MovieState> mapEventToState(MovieEvent
event) async* {
    if (event is FetchMovies) {
      yield MoviesLoading();

      try {
```

295

```
        // Simulating a network request
        await   Future.delayed(Duration(seconds:
2));

        final  movies  =  ["Movie  1",  "Movie  2",
"Movie 3"];
        yield MoviesLoaded(movies: movies);
      } catch (e) {
        yield  MoviesError(message:  "Failed  to
fetch movies");
      }
    }
  }
}
```

In this example:

- The **mapEventToState** method listens for the **FetchMovies** event and processes it.
- If the fetch is successful, it yields **MoviesLoaded** with a list of movie titles.
- If an error occurs, it yields **MoviesError**.

3. **Creating the UI**

Now, let's create the UI that listens for the states and displays the movies:

```
dart
```

```dart
// movie_screen.dart
import 'package:flutter/material.dart';
import 'package:flutter_bloc/flutter_bloc.dart';
import 'movie_bloc.dart';
import 'movie_event.dart';
import 'movie_state.dart';

class MovieScreen extends StatelessWidget {
  @override
  Widget build(BuildContext context) {
    return Scaffold(
      appBar: AppBar(title: Text("Movie App")),
      body: BlocProvider(
        create:            (context)              =>
MovieBloc()..add(FetchMovies()),
        child:             BlocBuilder<MovieBloc,
MovieState>(
          builder: (context, state) {
            if (state is MoviesLoading) {
              return              Center(child:
CircularProgressIndicator());
            }
            if (state is MoviesError) {
              return              Center(child:
Text(state.message));
            }
            if (state is MoviesLoaded) {
              return ListView.builder(
```

```
                itemCount: state.movies.length,
                itemBuilder: (context, index) {
                    return          ListTile(title:
Text(state.movies[index]));
                    },
                );
            }
            return     Center(child:     Text('No
data'));
            },
          ),
        ),
      );
    }
}
```

In this UI:

- We use **BlocProvider** to provide the **MovieBloc** to the widget tree.
- **BlocBuilder** listens for state changes and rebuilds the UI based on the current state.
  - **MoviesLoading**: Displays a loading indicator.
  - **MoviesError**: Displays an error message.
  - **MoviesLoaded**: Displays the list of movies.

Summary

In this chapter, we explored advanced state management solutions in Flutter:

- **Provider**, **Riverpod**, and **Bloc**: We compared their features and use cases, and learned when to use each one based on app complexity.
- **Bloc**: We went into detail about using Bloc for complex state management, including defining **events** and **states**, creating the **Bloc** class, and integrating it into the UI.
- **Real-World Example**: We built a **movie app** using Bloc for state management, handling the process of fetching movie data asynchronously and updating the UI based on state changes.

By using the appropriate state management solution, you can maintain clean, efficient, and scalable code, especially for large apps with complex logic and asynchronous data fetching.

CHAPTER 23

USING THIRD-PARTY PACKAGES AND PLUGINS

In Flutter, **third-party packages** and **plugins** play a crucial role in expanding the functionality of your app. Instead of reinventing the wheel, you can leverage community-created libraries and tools to handle tasks like networking, authentication, animations, and more. In this chapter, we will explain **what Flutter packages and plugins are**, how to **find and use third-party packages**, and we'll walk through a **real-world example** of adding **social media login** to your app using third-party plugins.

What Are Flutter Packages and Plugins?

In Flutter, **packages** are reusable libraries of code that you can include in your app to add specific functionality. **Plugins**, on the other hand, are packages that contain **platform-specific code** (iOS and Android) in addition to Dart code, allowing your app to interact with device APIs or other platform-specific functionality.

1. Flutter Packages

- **Pure Dart code**: These packages are written entirely in Dart and do not require platform-specific code. They can be used on any platform that Flutter supports (mobile, web, desktop).
- **Example**: Packages for data manipulation, JSON parsing, utilities like date formatting, etc.

2. Flutter Plugins

- **Platform-specific code**: These packages contain both Dart code and platform-specific code (for Android, iOS, etc.) to access native features of the device, such as camera access, GPS, or social media login.
- **Example**: Packages that use native APIs for accessing device sensors, camera, Bluetooth, or location services.

Flutter packages and plugins allow you to save time and effort by integrating pre-built solutions into your app, making it faster to build feature-rich apps.

How to Find and Use Third-Party Packages

1. Finding Packages on Pub.dev

Flutter has a package management system called **pub.dev** that hosts thousands of open-source packages and plugins. You can easily find and browse packages here.

- **Visit the Flutter Package Repository**: Go to pub.dev to search for Flutter packages.
- **Search for Packages**: You can search for packages based on functionality (e.g., "authentication," "networking," "camera") or by browsing categories.
- **Package Documentation**: Each package includes documentation on how to install and use it, as well as any dependencies or configuration needed.

2. Adding a Package to Your Project

To add a package to your Flutter project:

1. **Open pubspec.yaml**: This is where you define your project dependencies.
2. **Add the Package Dependency**: Under the dependencies section, add the package name and version number. For example, to use the firebase_auth package for Firebase authentication:

yaml

```
dependencies:
  flutter:
    sdk: flutter
  firebase_auth: ^3.1.0
```

3. **Install the Package**: After saving the changes to `pubspec.yaml`, run the following command in the terminal to fetch the package:

```bash
bash
```

```
flutter pub get
```

This will download and integrate the package into your project.

3. Importing the Package

Once the package is added to your project, you can import it in your Dart files and start using it:

```
dart
```

```
import
'package:firebase_auth/firebase_auth.dart';
```

Now you can access the features provided by the `firebase_auth` package.

Example: Adding Social Media Login to Your App Using Third-Party Plugins

Let's walk through a real-world example of integrating **social media login** (specifically **Google login**) into a Flutter app using the `google_sign_in` package, which is a third-party plugin.

Step 1: Adding Dependencies

1. Open your `pubspec.yaml` file and add the `google_sign_in` and `firebase_auth` plugins to your dependencies section:

yaml

```
dependencies:
  flutter:
    sdk: flutter
  google_sign_in: ^5.0.7
  firebase_auth: ^3.1.0
  firebase_core: ^1.10.0
```

2. Save the file and run `flutter pub get` to install the packages.

Step 2: Configuring Firebase

For Google Sign-In to work, you need to set up Firebase for your project:

1. Go to the Firebase Console, create a new project (or use an existing one).

2. Add your Flutter app to Firebase (for both Android and iOS).

3. Follow the instructions to integrate Firebase into your Flutter project:

   o For **Android**, add the **google-services.json** file to your `android/app` directory.

   o For **iOS**, add the **GoogleService-Info.plist** to your `ios/Runner` directory and ensure that the `firebase_core` and `google_sign_in` packages are configured.

Step 3: Implementing Google Sign-In

Now that Firebase is set up, let's implement Google login functionality in your app. Here's how to do it:

```dart
dart

import 'package:flutter/material.dart';
import
'package:google_sign_in/google_sign_in.dart';
import
'package:firebase_auth/firebase_auth.dart';

void main() {
  runApp(MyApp());
```

```dart
}

class MyApp extends StatelessWidget {
  @override
  Widget build(BuildContext context) {
    return MaterialApp(
      home: SignInScreen(),
    );
  }
}

class SignInScreen extends StatefulWidget {
  @override
  _SignInScreenState createState() =>
_SignInScreenState();
}

class _SignInScreenState extends
State<SignInScreen> {
  final GoogleSignIn _googleSignIn =
GoogleSignIn();
  final FirebaseAuth _auth =
FirebaseAuth.instance;

  // Method to handle Google Sign-In
  Future<User?> _signInWithGoogle() async {
    try {
      // Trigger the Google Sign-In flow
```

```
      final  GoogleSignInAccount?  googleUser  =
await _googleSignIn.signIn();
      final            GoogleSignInAuthentication
googleAuth = await googleUser!.authentication;

      // Create a new credential
      final   AuthCredential   credential   =
GoogleAuthProvider.credential(
        accessToken: googleAuth.accessToken,
        idToken: googleAuth.idToken,
      );

      // Sign in to Firebase with the credential
      final  UserCredential  userCredential  =
await _auth.signInWithCredential(credential);

      // Return the user object
      return userCredential.user;
    } catch (error) {
      print("Error  signing  in  with  Google:
$error");
      return null;
    }
  }

  // Method to handle sign-out
  Future<void> _signOut() async {
    await _googleSignIn.signOut();
    await _auth.signOut();
```

307

```
  }

  @override
  Widget build(BuildContext context) {
    return Scaffold(
      appBar: AppBar(title: Text('Google Sign-
In')),
      body: Center(
        child: Column(
          mainAxisAlignment:
MainAxisAlignment.center,
          children: [
            ElevatedButton(
              onPressed: () async {
                User? user = await
_signInWithGoogle();
                if (user != null) {
                  print('Signed in as
${user.displayName}');
                } else {
                  print('Sign-in failed');
                }
              },
              child: Text('Sign in with
Google'),
            ),
            ElevatedButton(
              onPressed: () async {
                await _signOut();
```

308

```
        print('Signed out');
      },
      child: Text('Sign out'),
    ),
  ],
),
),
);
}
}
```

Step 4: Explanation of the Code

- **GoogleSignIn**: This class manages the Google authentication process. It allows users to sign in with their Google account.

- **FirebaseAuth**: After successfully signing in with Google, we use **firebase_auth** to authenticate the user and sign them into Firebase.

- **Authentication Flow**:
  1. The user is prompted to sign in with Google.
  2. Once authenticated, we retrieve the user's credentials (access token and ID token) and use them to authenticate with Firebase.
  3. After successful authentication, we return the **Firebase User** object.

Step 5: Running the App

1. After implementing the code, run your app on an Android or iOS device.

2. Click the **Sign in with Google** button to authenticate with Google.

3. If the sign-in is successful, the user will be signed in, and their information will be displayed in the console.

Conclusion

In this chapter, we explored how to use **third-party packages** and **plugins** in Flutter to enhance the functionality of your app. Specifically, we covered:

- **What Flutter packages and plugins are** and how they extend Flutter's capabilities.

- **How to find and use third-party packages** via **pub.dev** and add them to your project.

- A **real-world example** of adding **Google sign-in** to your app using the `google_sign_in` plugin, with Firebase authentication for backend integration.

By using third-party packages and plugins, you can significantly reduce development time, leverage community-driven solutions, and add powerful features to your app with minimal effort.

CHAPTER 24

SECURITY BEST PRACTICES IN FLUTTER APPS

In this chapter, we will focus on security best practices in Flutter apps, ensuring that user data is protected, and authentication mechanisms are secure. Flutter provides a variety of tools and techniques to enhance security and protect sensitive data. We will discuss how to secure sensitive information, use secure storage for data, and implement secure user authentication. We will also build an example of a **secure login system** that follows industry-standard security practices.

Protecting Sensitive Data in Flutter Apps

When developing a mobile app, protecting sensitive data, such as passwords, personal information, or financial details, is critical. If this data is compromised, it can lead to serious security issues, including data breaches and identity theft.

Here are some general principles for protecting sensitive data in Flutter apps:

1. Encrypt Sensitive Data

Encrypt sensitive data before storing it locally, even if you're using secure storage. Encryption ensures that even if data is accessed by unauthorized parties, it cannot be read without the decryption key.

- **AES (Advanced Encryption Standard)** is a commonly used symmetric encryption algorithm for encrypting sensitive data.
- Use the `encrypt` package to handle encryption and decryption in Flutter.

2. Avoid Storing Sensitive Data in Plain Text

Never store sensitive information like passwords, tokens, or private keys in plain text, either in **SharedPreferences**, **SQLite**, or files. Always use secure storage or encrypted files.

3. Use Secure Storage Solutions

Flutter offers plugins like `flutter_secure_storage` to securely store sensitive data, such as tokens or passwords, in the device's secure storage.

4. HTTPS for Network Communication

Always use **HTTPS** instead of HTTP for network requests to protect data in transit. This encrypts the data being sent between the client and server, ensuring that third parties cannot intercept sensitive information.

5. Handle User Authentication Securely

User authentication should be performed securely, ideally using **OAuth** or **Firebase Authentication**, and sensitive credentials should not be stored on the device. Use token-based authentication (JWT tokens) for secure communication.

Secure Storage Using the `flutter_secure_storage` Plugin

One of the most common methods to store sensitive data in a Flutter app is to use the `flutter_secure_storage` plugin. This plugin provides a way to store key-value pairs in a secure storage area on both Android and iOS, which is encrypted by default.

Step 1: Adding the Dependency

First, add the `flutter_secure_storage` package to your `pubspec.yaml` file:

```yaml
yaml

dependencies:
  flutter:
    sdk: flutter
  flutter_secure_storage: ^5.0.2
```

Then, run `flutter pub get` to install the plugin.

Step 2: Using `flutter_secure_storage`

Now, let's use **flutter_secure_storage** to store and retrieve sensitive data. The plugin allows you to securely store values such as passwords or API keys.

```dart
dart

import
'package:flutter_secure_storage/flutter_secure_
storage.dart';

final _secureStorage = FlutterSecureStorage();

// Saving a value securely
Future<void> saveData(String key, String value)
async {
  await _secureStorage.write(key: key, value:
value);
}
```

```
// Reading a value securely
Future<String?> getData(String key) async {
  return await _secureStorage.read(key: key);
}

// Deleting a value securely
Future<void> deleteData(String key) async {
  await _secureStorage.delete(key: key);
}
```

In this example:

- **write()**: Saves data securely.
- **read()**: Reads the stored data.
- **delete()**: Deletes the stored data.

The data is encrypted on both Android (using the **Keychain** on iOS and **Keystore** on Android), ensuring that it is stored safely.

Best Practices for Secure User Authentication

User authentication is one of the most critical aspects of security in a mobile app. Here are some best practices to follow when implementing secure authentication:

315

1. Use OAuth or OpenID Connect

For secure authentication, use **OAuth** or **OpenID Connect** to handle token-based authentication, which provides more security than traditional username and password-based authentication.

- **OAuth** allows third-party services (like Google, Facebook, or GitHub) to authenticate users without exposing their passwords.
- **OpenID Connect** builds on OAuth, adding authentication to it (user identity).

2. Implement Multi-Factor Authentication (MFA)

Multi-factor authentication (MFA) adds an extra layer of security by requiring users to provide something they know (password) and something they have (an SMS code, an app authenticator, or a hardware token).

3. Use Firebase Authentication

Firebase Authentication provides a secure and easy way to handle authentication in Flutter apps. It supports various authentication methods, including email/password authentication, Google sign-in, Facebook login, and phone number verification.

4. Secure Password Storage

Never store user passwords directly on the device or in plain text. Always hash the password before storing it in the database. Use a strong hashing algorithm such as **PBKDF2 or bcrypt**.

5. Token-Based Authentication

Use **JWT (JSON Web Tokens)** or **OAuth tokens** for authentication. These tokens are more secure because they don't require you to store sensitive credentials on the device. Tokens can be used to authenticate the user and authorize their access to certain resources.

Example: Creating a Secure Login System

Let's create a simple **secure login system** using **Firebase Authentication** for authentication and **flutter_secure_storage** to store the authentication token securely.

Step 1: Adding Dependencies

Add the required dependencies in your `pubspec.yaml`:

```yaml
dependencies:
```

```
flutter:
  sdk: flutter
firebase_core: ^1.10.0
firebase_auth: ^3.1.0
flutter_secure_storage: ^5.0.2
```

Step 2: Setting Up Firebase Authentication

Before we proceed with the code, ensure you've set up Firebase in your Flutter project by following the steps in the Firebase documentation. This includes adding Firebase to both your Android and iOS project and configuring authentication methods.

Step 3: Writing the Login Code

Here's how you can implement a secure login system:

dart

```dart
import 'package:flutter/material.dart';
import
'package:firebase_auth/firebase_auth.dart';
import
'package:flutter_secure_storage/flutter_secure_
storage.dart';
import
'package:firebase_core/firebase_core.dart';

final _firebaseAuth = FirebaseAuth.instance;
final _secureStorage = FlutterSecureStorage();
```

318

```
void main() async {
  WidgetsFlutterBinding.ensureInitialized();
  await Firebase.initializeApp();  // Initialize
Firebase
  runApp(MyApp());
}

class MyApp extends StatelessWidget {
  @override
  Widget build(BuildContext context) {
    return MaterialApp(
      home: LoginPage(),
    );
  }
}

class LoginPage extends StatefulWidget {
  @override
  _LoginPageState       createState()          =>
_LoginPageState();
}

class _LoginPageState extends State<LoginPage> {
  final TextEditingController _emailController =
TextEditingController();
  final              TextEditingController
_passwordController = TextEditingController();
```

```dart
// Sign in method
Future<void> _signInWithEmailPassword() async
{
  try {
    // Authenticate the user
    UserCredential userCredential = await
_firebaseAuth.signInWithEmailAndPassword(
      email: _emailController.text,
      password: _passwordController.text,
    );

    // Store the user's authentication token
securely
    String? token = await
userCredential.user?.getIdToken();
    if (token != null) {
      await _secureStorage.write(key:
'authToken', value: token);
    }

    print("User signed in successfully!");

  } catch (e) {
    print("Error signing in: $e");
  }
}

// Sign out method
Future<void> _signOut() async {
```

```
  await _firebaseAuth.signOut();
  await           _secureStorage.delete(key:
'authToken');
  print("User signed out successfully!");
}


@override
Widget build(BuildContext context) {
  return Scaffold(
    appBar:     AppBar(title:     Text('Secure
Login')),
    body: Padding(
      padding: const EdgeInsets.all(16.0),
      child: Column(
        children: [
          TextField(
            controller: _emailController,
            decoration:
InputDecoration(labelText: 'Email'),
          ),
          TextField(
            controller: _passwordController,
            obscureText: true,
            decoration:
InputDecoration(labelText: 'Password'),
          ),
          SizedBox(height: 20),
          ElevatedButton(
```

```
              onPressed:
_signInWithEmailPassword,
            child: Text('Sign In'),
          ),
          ElevatedButton(
            onPressed: _signOut,
            child: Text('Sign Out'),
          ),
        ],
      ),
    ),
  );
  }
}
```

Explanation:

1. **Firebase Authentication**: We use **signInWithEmailAndPassword** to authenticate the user using their email and password.

2. **flutter_secure_storage**: After successful login, we store the **authentication token** securely using **flutter_secure_storage**.

3. **Sign Out**: When the user logs out, we delete the authentication token from secure storage to prevent unauthorized access.

Step 4: Running the App

1. After implementing the code, run your app on an Android or iOS device.
2. Enter the email and password and click **Sign In**.
3. The app will authenticate the user, store the token securely, and display the sign-out button.

Summary

In this chapter, we covered essential security best practices for Flutter apps, including:

- **Protecting sensitive data** by using encryption, secure storage, and avoiding plain-text storage.
- **Using flutter_secure_storage** to store sensitive information, such as authentication tokens, securely.
- **Best practices for user authentication**, such as using token-based authentication, OAuth, and multi-factor authentication (MFA).
- A **real-world example** of creating a **secure login system** using **Firebase Authentication** and **flutter_secure_storage**.

By following these best practices, you can significantly enhance the security of your Flutter apps and ensure that user data is protected from potential threats.

CHAPTER 25

INTERNATIONALIZATION AND LOCALIZATION

In this chapter, we will explore the concepts of **internationalization** (i18n) and **localization** (l10n) in Flutter apps. These two concepts allow you to make your app accessible and usable in different languages and regions, making it a crucial step in expanding your app's reach to a global audience. We will look at Flutter's built-in localization features, how to translate your app into multiple languages, and build an example of a **multi-language shopping app**.

What is Localization in Mobile Apps?

Localization (l10n) is the process of adapting your app to different languages and cultural settings. This includes:

- Translating the text content of the app into multiple languages.
- Adjusting the design and layout to accommodate languages with different character sets and reading directions (e.g., right-to-left for Arabic or Hebrew).

- Formatting numbers, dates, times, and currencies according to the region's conventions.

Localization ensures that users in different regions can interact with your app as if it were specifically designed for their language and culture.

Internationalization (i18n) vs. Localization (l10n):

- **Internationalization (i18n)** is the process of preparing your app to handle multiple languages and regions. This involves structuring your app in such a way that it can be easily translated and adapted to various languages without modifying the codebase extensively.
- **Localization (l10n)** is the actual process of translating the app and adapting it to a specific locale (region or language).

Using Flutter's Built-in Localization Features

Flutter provides **built-in support** for both **internationalization (i18n)** and **localization (l10n)** via the `intl` package, making it easier to create apps that can adapt to multiple languages.

Step 1: Adding Dependencies

To get started, you'll need to add the necessary dependencies in your `pubspec.yaml` file:

```yaml
dependencies:
  flutter:
    sdk: flutter
  intl: ^0.17.0  # Add intl package for internationalization support

dev_dependencies:
  flutter_localizations:
    sdk: flutter
```

After adding the dependencies, run the following command to install them:

```bash
flutter pub get
```

Step 2: Enabling Localization in Your App

1. **Add localization delegates** to your `MaterialApp` widget: Flutter has built-in support for different locales, such as **English (en)**, **Spanish (es)**, and **French (fr)**, using **flutter_localizations**.

327

```dart
dart

import
'package:flutter_localizations/flutter_localiza
tions.dart';

void main() {
  runApp(MyApp());
}

class MyApp extends StatelessWidget {
  @override
  Widget build(BuildContext context) {
    return MaterialApp(
      title: 'Multi-language Shopping App',
      supportedLocales: [
        Locale('en', ''), // English
        Locale('es', ''), // Spanish
        Locale('fr', ''), // French
      ],
      localizationsDelegates: [
        GlobalMaterialLocalizations.delegate,
        GlobalWidgetsLocalizations.delegate,
        GlobalCupertinoLocalizations.delegate,
      ],
      home: ShoppingPage(),
    );
  }
}
```

- **supportedLocales**: Specifies the locales that your app supports (e.g., English, Spanish, French).

- **localizationsDelegates**: Provides the necessary delegates to load the localized resources for Material widgets, Cupertino widgets, and general localization.

Translating Your App into Multiple Languages

After setting up the necessary dependencies and localization delegates, the next step is to create the translated content for your app.

Step 1: Creating Localization Files

Flutter uses `.arb` (Application Resource Bundle) files to store the translated strings. These files are simple JSON-like files that contain key-value pairs where the key is the string identifier and the value is the localized translation.

1. Create a folder called `lib/l10n/` in your project directory.

2. Inside this folder, create two `.arb` files for the English and Spanish languages:

- **intl_en.arb** (for English):

json

```json
{
  "title": "Shopping App",
  "welcome": "Welcome to our shopping app!",
  "shopNow": "Shop Now"
}
```

- **intl_es.arb** (for Spanish):

json

```json
{
  "title": "Aplicación de Compras",
  "welcome": "¡Bienvenido a nuestra aplicación de compras!",
  "shopNow": "Comprar Ahora"
}
```

Step 2: Generating Localization Code

Flutter provides a command to generate Dart code from your .arb files. To generate this code:

1. In your terminal, run the following command:

bash

```bash
flutter pub run intl_utils:generate
```

2. This command will create a file called `l10n.dart` that contains a class for each string in your `.arb` files, such as:

```dart
class AppLocalizations {
  static   AppLocalizations?   of(BuildContext context) {
    return
Localizations.of<AppLocalizations>(context,
AppLocalizations);
  }

  String get title => Intl.message('Shopping App', name: 'title');
  String get welcome => Intl.message('Welcome to our shopping app!', name: 'welcome');
  String get shopNow => Intl.message('Shop Now', name: 'shopNow');
}
```

Step 3: Accessing Translated Text in Your App

Once the generated localization code is available, you can access the translated text in your app.

```dart
import 'package:flutter/material.dart';
```

```dart
import
'package:flutter_localizations/flutter_localiza
tions.dart';

class ShoppingPage extends StatelessWidget {
  @override
  Widget build(BuildContext context) {
    // Access localized strings using
AppLocalizations.of(context)
    final AppLocalizations localizations =
AppLocalizations.of(context)!;

    return Scaffold(
      appBar: AppBar(
        title: Text(localizations.title),
      ),
      body: Column(
        mainAxisAlignment:
MainAxisAlignment.center,
        children: [
          Text(localizations.welcome),
          ElevatedButton(
            onPressed: () {},
            child: Text(localizations.shopNow),
          ),
        ],
      ),
    );
  }
```

332

```
}
```

This example shows how to display localized strings for the app title, welcome message, and button label in the UI.

Example: Creating a Multi-Language Shopping App

Let's build a simple **multi-language shopping app** with support for English and Spanish. The app will display a **welcome message**, a **title**, and a **"Shop Now"** button in different languages based on the user's locale.

Step 1: Setting up the Localization Files

We have already created the `intl_en.arb` and `intl_es.arb` files with the translations for the **welcome message, title**, and **shop button**.

Step 2: Configuring Localization in `MaterialApp`

Update the `MaterialApp` widget to support multiple locales and the corresponding translations.

```dart
import 'package:flutter/material.dart';
```

```dart
import
'package:flutter_localizations/flutter_localiza
tions.dart';
import 'l10n.dart';   // Generated localization
code

void main() {
  runApp(MyApp());
}

class MyApp extends StatelessWidget {
  @override
  Widget build(BuildContext context) {
    return MaterialApp(
      title: 'Multi-language Shopping App',
      supportedLocales: [
        Locale('en', ''), // English
        Locale('es', ''), // Spanish
      ],
      localizationsDelegates: [
        GlobalMaterialLocalizations.delegate,
        GlobalWidgetsLocalizations.delegate,
        GlobalCupertinoLocalizations.delegate,
        AppLocalizations.delegate,   // Delegate
for custom localization
      ],
      home: ShoppingPage(),
    );
  }
```

```
}
```

Step 3: Using Localized Strings

Now, let's use the localized strings in the `ShoppingPage`:

dart

```dart
class ShoppingPage extends StatelessWidget {
  @override
  Widget build(BuildContext context) {
    final AppLocalizations localizations =
AppLocalizations.of(context)!;

    return Scaffold(
      appBar: AppBar(
        title: Text(localizations.title),
      ),
      body: Column(
        mainAxisAlignment:
MainAxisAlignment.center,
        children: [
          Text(localizations.welcome),
          ElevatedButton(
            onPressed: () {},
            child: Text(localizations.shopNow),
          ),
        ],
      ),
    );
```

```
    }
}
```

Step 4: Testing the App

1. **Change the Language**: On your Android or iOS device, change the language of the device to either **English** or **Spanish**.

2. Run your app, and the **welcome message**, **title**, and **button text** should automatically update based on the device's language setting.

Summary

In this chapter, we covered:

- **Localization** in mobile apps, which enables you to provide a tailored experience for users in different languages and regions.

- **Flutter's built-in localization features**, such as the flutter_localizations package and **intl** package for handling multi-language apps.

- **Creating a multi-language shopping app** by defining **localized strings**, setting up **MaterialApp** for locale support, and using the generated **AppLocalizations** class to access translations.

By following these practices, you can build a Flutter app that is **internationalized** and **localized**, providing a more inclusive and user-friendly experience for users across the globe.

CHAPTER 26

REAL-WORLD CASE STUDY: BUILDING A FULL-FEATURED APP

In this chapter, we'll walk through the process of building a **real-world task manager app** using **Flutter**. This will combine everything we've learned so far, from building the UI, managing state, integrating networking features, and adding local storage. The goal is to showcase how all these concepts come together to create a full-featured app.

We'll cover:

1. **App Requirements**: What features we need for the app.
2. **Setting Up the Project**: How to set up the Flutter project.
3. **Building the UI**: Designing the task manager interface.
4. **State Management**: Using state management to handle app data.
5. **Networking**: Fetching data from a remote server.
6. **Local Storage**: Saving data locally for offline access.
7. **Putting It All Together**: Finalizing the app with all features working.

By the end of this chapter, you'll have a complete task manager app that combines all the tools and techniques you've learned in Flutter development.

App Requirements

Before we start coding, let's define the key features our task manager app will have:

1. **Task List**: Display a list of tasks with titles, descriptions, and due dates.
2. **Add/Remove Tasks**: Add new tasks to the list and remove completed tasks.
3. **Task Status**: Mark tasks as completed or pending.
4. **Local Storage**: Store tasks locally so they persist across app sessions.
5. **Networking**: Integrate with a simple backend API to fetch and update tasks.

With these requirements in mind, let's get started!

Step 1: Setting Up the Project

1. **Create a new Flutter project**:

   Open a terminal and run:

```bash
bash
```

```bash
flutter create task_manager_app
cd task_manager_app
```

2. **Install dependencies**:

Open the `pubspec.yaml` file and add the following dependencies:

```yaml
yaml
```

```yaml
dependencies:
  flutter:
    sdk: flutter
  provider: ^6.0.1
  http: ^0.14.0
  flutter_secure_storage: ^5.0.2
  intl: ^0.17.0
```

These packages will help with:

- o **State management**: provider
- o **Networking**: http
- o **Local storage**: flutter_secure_storage
- o **Date and time formatting**: intl

After adding these, run `flutter pub get` to install the dependencies.

340

Step 2: Building the UI

Let's create the basic UI for the task manager app. We'll need:

- A task list view to display tasks.
- A form to add new tasks.
- A way to mark tasks as completed.

Main App Structure

Start by creating the `main.dart` file to structure the app:

dart

```dart
import 'package:flutter/material.dart';
import 'package:provider/provider.dart';
import 'task_model.dart';
import 'task_provider.dart';
import 'task_screen.dart';

void main() {
  runApp(MyApp());
}

class MyApp extends StatelessWidget {
  @override
  Widget build(BuildContext context) {
    return ChangeNotifierProvider(
```

341

```
    create: (context) => TaskProvider(),
    child: MaterialApp(
      title: 'Task Manager App',
      theme: ThemeData(
        primarySwatch: Colors.blue,
      ),
      home: TaskScreen(),
    ),
  );
}
}
```

Here:

- We use `ChangeNotifierProvider` to provide the `TaskProvider` to the app, which will manage the app's state.
- The `TaskScreen` widget is the main screen that will display the task list and handle task interactions.

Task List UI

Next, we need a screen to display the list of tasks. Create a new file `task_screen.dart`:

dart

```
import 'package:flutter/material.dart';
import 'package:provider/provider.dart';
```

342

```dart
import 'task_provider.dart';
import 'task_model.dart';

class TaskScreen extends StatelessWidget {
  @override
  Widget build(BuildContext context) {
    final            taskProvider            =
Provider.of<TaskProvider>(context);

    return Scaffold(
      appBar:      AppBar(title:      Text('Task
Manager')),
      body: ListView.builder(
        itemCount: taskProvider.tasks.length,
        itemBuilder: (context, index) {
          final              task              =
taskProvider.tasks[index];
          return ListTile(
            title: Text(task.title),
            subtitle: Text(task.description),
            trailing: Checkbox(
              value: task.isCompleted,
              onChanged: (value) {

taskProvider.toggleTaskCompletion(task.id);
              },
            ),
            onLongPress: () {
              taskProvider.deleteTask(task.id);
```

```
                },
              );
            },
          ),
        floatingActionButton:
FloatingActionButton(
            onPressed: () {
              _showAddTaskDialog(context);
            },
            child: Icon(Icons.add),
          ),
      );
  }


  void _showAddTaskDialog(BuildContext context)
{
    showDialog(
      context: context,
      builder: (BuildContext context) {
        final         titleController         =
TextEditingController();
        final    descriptionController         =
TextEditingController();


        return AlertDialog(
          title: Text('Add New Task'),
          content: Column(
            children: [
              TextField(
```

```
          controller: titleController,
          decoration:
InputDecoration(labelText: 'Title'),
          ),
          TextField(
          controller:
descriptionController,
          decoration:
InputDecoration(labelText: 'Description'),
          ),
        ],
      ),
      actions: [
        TextButton(
        onPressed: () {
          final          title          =
titleController.text;
          final          description          =
descriptionController.text;
          if     (title.isNotEmpty     &&
description.isNotEmpty) {

Provider.of<TaskProvider>(context,          listen:
false)
                  .addTask(title,
description);
              Navigator.pop(context);
            }
          },
```

```
            child: Text('Add'),
          ),
        ],
      );
    },
  );
 }
}
```

This screen includes:

- A **task list** displayed in a `ListView` with a **Checkbox** to mark tasks as completed.
- A **FloatingActionButton** that opens a dialog to add a new task.
- When a task is long-pressed, it is deleted from the list.

Step 3: State Management with Provider

Now, let's implement the **state management** for our app. The `TaskProvider` will manage the state of the tasks, including adding, deleting, and updating tasks.

Create a new file `task_provider.dart`:

dart

```
import 'package:flutter/material.dart';
```

```dart
import 'task_model.dart';

class TaskProvider with ChangeNotifier {
  List<Task> _tasks = [];

  List<Task> get tasks => _tasks;

  void addTask(String title, String description)
{
    final newTask = Task(
      id: DateTime.now().toString(),
      title: title,
      description: description,
      isCompleted: false,
    );
    _tasks.add(newTask);
    notifyListeners();
  }

  void deleteTask(String id) {
    _tasks.removeWhere((task) => task.id == id);
    notifyListeners();
  }

  void toggleTaskCompletion(String id) {
    final task = _tasks.firstWhere((task)   =>
task.id == id);
    task.isCompleted = !task.isCompleted;
    notifyListeners();
```

```
    }
}
```

In this provider:

- **addTask** adds a new task to the list.
- **deleteTask** removes a task by its ID.
- **toggleTaskCompletion** changes the task's completion status (from pending to completed).

Step 4: Task Model

Create a file `task_model.dart` to define the task model:

dart

```dart
class Task {
  final String id;
  final String title;
  final String description;
  bool isCompleted;

  Task({
    required this.id,
    required this.title,
    required this.description,
    this.isCompleted = false,
  });
```

```
}
```

This model represents a task, including its id, title, description, and isCompleted status.

Step 5: Networking – Fetching and Saving Data

For the networking part, let's assume you're connecting to a backend API to fetch and save tasks. You can use the http package to make network requests.

dart

```dart
import 'package:http/http.dart' as http;
import 'dart:convert';

Future<void> fetchTasks() async {
  final response = await http.get(Uri.parse('https://your-api-
url.com/tasks'));
  if (response.statusCode == 200) {
    List<dynamic> data = json.decode(response.body);
    // Parse and add tasks to the provider
  } else {
    throw Exception('Failed to load tasks');
  }
}
```

```dart
Future<void> addTaskToServer(String title,
String description) async {
  final response = await http.post(
    Uri.parse('https://your-api-
url.com/tasks'),
    body: json.encode({
      'title': title,
      'description': description,
    }),
  );
  if (response.statusCode != 200) {
    throw Exception('Failed to add task');
  }
}
```

You can integrate these methods into your `TaskProvider` to fetch and save tasks from the backend.

Step 6: Local Storage

To persist tasks locally, you can use the **flutter_secure_storage** plugin to securely store the task data. You can save the task list as a JSON string and retrieve it on app launch.

dart

```
import
'package:flutter_secure_storage/flutter_secure_
storage.dart';

final _secureStorage = FlutterSecureStorage();

Future<void> saveTasksLocally(List<Task> tasks)
async {
  final tasksJson = json.encode(tasks.map((task)
=> task.toJson()).toList());
  await    _secureStorage.write(key:    'tasks',
value: tasksJson);
}

Future<List<Task>> loadTasksLocally() async {
  final        tasksJson        =        await
_secureStorage.read(key: 'tasks');
  if (tasksJson != null) {
    List<dynamic> data = json.decode(tasksJson);
    return          data.map((task)          =>
Task.fromJson(task)).toList();
  }
  return [];
}
```

In this example:

- **saveTasksLocally** stores the tasks securely in the device.

- **loadTasksLocally** loads the tasks when the app starts.

Step 7: Putting It All Together

Now that we have the core functionalities, we can combine everything:

- UI to display tasks.
- Provider to manage app state.
- Networking to fetch and save data.
- Local storage for offline access.

You now have a full-featured task manager app built using Flutter, with the following features:

- Task list with add, remove, and mark as completed actions.
- State management with **Provider**.
- Networking to fetch and save tasks from a backend API.
- Local storage to persist data for offline access.

Summary

In this chapter, we built a **task manager app** using **Flutter**. The app incorporated:

- **UI development**: Designing screens and using Flutter widgets.
- **State management**: Using **Provider** to manage app data.
- **Networking**: Fetching and saving data from/to a backend API.
- **Local storage**: Storing data locally using **flutter_secure_storage**.

This real-world case study shows how to combine various Flutter concepts to build a fully functional app, ready for both online and offline use.

CHAPTER 27

FUTURE OF FLUTTER AND THE MOBILE DEVELOPMENT LANDSCAPE

In this final chapter, we'll look at the future of **Flutter** and its potential to shape the mobile development landscape in the coming years. Flutter's growth has been exponential, and its ability to target multiple platforms makes it a strong contender for the future of app development. We'll explore what's next for Flutter, its expansion into web, desktop, and embedded devices, and provide some final thoughts and best practices for becoming a proficient Flutter developer.

What's Next for Flutter?

Flutter has gained significant momentum since its launch, and Google continues to actively develop and improve the framework. Some of the areas where we can expect significant progress include:

1. Flutter for Web and Desktop

- **Flutter Web**: Initially, Flutter was focused on mobile app development, but **Flutter for Web** is making huge strides. It allows you to build responsive, high-performance web apps using the same codebase that powers your mobile app. Though still in the beta stage, the **Flutter Web** team has made continuous improvements, and in the future, we can expect it to become a more stable and feature-rich option for developers.

- **Flutter Desktop**: Flutter has expanded to support building apps for **macOS**, **Windows**, and **Linux**. Although still maturing, **Flutter Desktop** provides developers the ability to target multiple platforms with a single codebase, making it a game-changer for cross-platform development.

2. Embedded Systems and IoT Devices

- **Flutter for Embedded Devices**: Flutter is also making its way into **embedded systems** and **IoT devices**. This is a fascinating area that opens up possibilities for building apps for devices that are not traditionally considered part of the mobile or desktop ecosystem (e.g., smart TVs, wearables, automotive systems). Google has already begun exploring Flutter's use in this space, and we can expect more tools and documentation in the near future to support this trend.

3. Improved Performance and Tooling

- **Performance Optimization**: As Flutter continues to mature, developers can expect even more improvements in performance, particularly in complex UI rendering and animations. Google's ongoing focus on **Flutter Engine** optimizations will make the framework even faster and more efficient.
- **Enhanced Development Tools**: Flutter's development tooling will also evolve. The **Flutter DevTools** suite will continue to grow, with better debugging tools, performance analyzers, and more advanced features to support developers in building and maintaining large-scale apps.

4. Flutter for Everything: A Unified Approach

The long-term vision for **Flutter** is to provide a unified framework that enables developers to create applications for **mobile, web, desktop, embedded devices**, and even **IoT**. This holistic approach is set to make Flutter the go-to solution for cross-platform development, allowing you to build apps for virtually any platform from a single codebase.

Flutter for the Future: Web, Desktop, and Embedded Devices

As Flutter evolves, the potential to target a wide variety of platforms continues to grow. Let's take a closer look at Flutter's expanding reach:

1. Flutter for Web

- **Current Status**: Flutter for Web is still in active development, but many developers are already experimenting with it. It's particularly useful for building **progressive web apps (PWAs)**, **single-page applications (SPAs)**, and **web apps** that need to provide a high-performance user experience.
- **The Future**: With enhanced tooling and optimization, we can expect Flutter Web to become even more stable and feature-rich, allowing developers to create **production-ready** web applications.

2. Flutter for Desktop

- **Current Status**: Flutter for Desktop is still in an experimental phase, but it's already being used in production by some companies. Developers can build desktop applications for **Windows**, **macOS**, and **Linux** using Flutter, which significantly reduces development time.

357

- **The Future**: As Flutter for Desktop becomes more stable, expect greater adoption by developers who want to target all platforms with one codebase. The integration of desktop-specific plugins (such as file system access, native menus, etc.) will be a key area of improvement.

3. Flutter for Embedded Devices

- **Current Status**: Flutter is beginning to expand into the world of **embedded devices** like **smart home devices**, **wearables**, and **automotive applications**. Flutter's flexibility and high-performance rendering engine make it ideal for these use cases.
- **The Future**: As embedded systems become more popular, Flutter's presence in the IoT space will increase. Expect official support and tooling to make Flutter a viable option for embedded app development.

Final Thoughts and Best Practices for Flutter Developers

As you continue to build and expand your skills as a Flutter developer, here are some **best practices** and tips to keep in mind:

1. Keep Learning and Stay Updated

Flutter is evolving rapidly, with new features and improvements being added regularly. Stay updated with the latest releases, best practices, and tools. Follow Flutter's official documentation, blogs, and the Flutter community to keep your knowledge fresh.

2. Master State Management

State management is one of the most challenging parts of Flutter development. Learn the different state management techniques (such as **Provider**, **Riverpod**, **Bloc**, etc.) and choose the one that fits your app's complexity. Having a solid understanding of state management will make your Flutter apps more scalable and maintainable.

3. Write Modular and Reusable Code

Flutter encourages a **declarative UI** approach, and modularity is key to building scalable apps. Break your app into smaller, reusable widgets, and ensure that your code is easy to maintain and test. This will improve the development process and make your app more maintainable in the long run.

4. Focus on Performance

As your app grows, performance becomes more important. Always keep performance in mind when building complex UIs or handling large amounts of data. Use tools like **Flutter DevTools** to monitor app performance and optimize your code for smoother user experiences.

5. Test Your Apps Thoroughly

Testing is essential for any serious app. Make use of Flutter's built-in testing capabilities, including **unit tests**, **widget tests**, and **integration tests**, to ensure your app behaves as expected across different scenarios.

Conclusion: Becoming a Proficient Flutter Developer

The future of Flutter is incredibly promising. With its growing support for web, desktop, and embedded devices, Flutter is poised to become the leading framework for cross-platform development. As a Flutter developer, you have the opportunity to be part of this exciting journey, creating apps that can run on mobile, web, desktop, and even embedded systems.

To become a proficient Flutter developer, focus on:

- Mastering the core concepts of Flutter, including **widgets**, **state management**, and **navigation**.
- Continuously improving your understanding of best practices and new features in Flutter.
- Building real-world projects to hone your skills and stay up-to-date with the latest trends.

By following these best practices, staying committed to learning, and embracing the growing Flutter ecosystem, you can position yourself as a proficient Flutter developer ready to build the next generation of cross-platform apps.

Summary

In this chapter, we:

- Explored **what's next for Flutter** and how it's expanding to **web, desktop**, and **embedded devices**.
- Discussed **Flutter's future** and its potential to become a unified solution for building apps across all platforms.
- Provided **best practices** for becoming a proficient Flutter developer, including learning state management, modular development, performance optimization, and testing.

With Flutter's continued growth and support from the development community, it's clear that **Flutter** is here to stay. Now is the perfect time to dive in and become part of this exciting journey!